Acknowledgements

The front cover illustration shows *Vanity Fair*, a painting of Charles Stewart Parnell (1880), Mary Evans Picture Library.

The publishers would like to thank the following for permission to reproduce illustrations in this volume:
Michael Nicholson/Corbis, page 32; The Mansell Collection, page 43; Hulton-Deutsch, page 65; Hulton-Deutsch/Corbis, page 78; Mary Evans Picture Library, page 85; The Illustrated London News Picture Library, page 98; Trustees of the National Museum and Galleries of Northern Ireland, page 119; Sean Sexton/Corbis, page 131.

Every effort has been made to trace and acknowledge ownership of copyright. The publishers will be glad to make arrangements with any copyright holders with whom it has not been possible to contact.

Orders: please contact Bookpoint Ltd, 130 Milton Park, Abingdon, Oxon OX14 4SB. Telephone: (44) 01235 827720, Fax: (44) 01235 400454. Lines are open from 9.00–6.00, Monday to Saturday, with a 24 hour message answering service. Email address: orders@bookpoint.co.uk

British Library Cataloguing in Publication Data
A catalogue record for this title is available from The British Library

ISBN 0 340 78948 4

First published 2001
Impression number 10 9 8 7 6 5 4 3
Year   2006 2005 2004 2003 2002

Typeset by Fakenham Photosetting Ltd, Fakenham, Norfolk.
Printed in Great Britain for Hodder & Stoughton Educational, a division of Hodder Headline Plc, 338 Euston Road, London NW1 3BH by Bath Press Ltd, England

acce *istory*

GREAT BRITAIN
AND THE IRISH
QUESTION
1800–1922

Second Edition

Paul Adelman and

Robert Pearce

Hodder & Stoughton

A MEMBER OF THE HODDER HEADLINE GROUP

Contents

Preface

To the general reader

Although the *Access to History* series has been designed with the needs of students studying the subject at higher examination levels very much in mind, it also has a great deal to offer the general reader. The main body of the text (i.e. ignoring the 'Study Guides' at the ends of chapters) forms a readable and yet stimulating survey of a coherent topic as studied by historians. However, each author's aim has not merely been to provide a clear explanation of what happened in the past (to interest and inform): it has also been assumed that most readers wish to be stimulated into thinking further about the topic and to form opinions of their own about the significance of the events that are described and discussed (to be challenged). Thus, although no prior knowledge of the topic is expected on the reader's part, she or he is treated as an intelligent and thinking person throughout. The author tends to share ideas and possibilities with the reader, rather than passing on numbers of so-called 'historical truths'.

To the student reader

Although advantage has been taken of the publication of a second edition to ensure the results of recent research are reflected in the text, the main alteration from the first edition is the inclusion of new features, and the modification of existing ones, aimed at assisting you in your study of the topic at AS level, A level and Higher. Two features are designed to assist you during your first reading of a chapter. The *Points to Consider* section following each chapter title is intended to focus your attention on the main theme(s) of the chapter, and the issues box following most section headings alerts you to the question or questions to be dealt with in the section. The *Working on...* section at the end of each chapter suggests ways of gaining maximum benefit from the chapter.

There are many ways in which the series can be used by students studying History at a higher level. It will, therefore, be worthwhile thinking about your own study strategy before you start your work on this book. Obviously, your strategy will vary depending on the aim you have in mind, and the time for study that is available to you.

If, for example, you want to acquire a general overview of the topic in the shortest possible time, the following approach will probably be the most effective:

1 Read chapter 1. As you do so, keep in mind the issues raised in the *Points to Consider* section.
2 Read the *Points to Consider* section at the beginning of chapter 2 and decide whether it is necessary for you to read this chapter.

3 If it is, read the chapter, stopping at each heading or sub-heading to note down the main points that have been made. Often, the best way of doing this is to answer the question(s) posed in the Key Issues boxes.

4 Repeat stage 2 (and stage 3 where appropriate) for all the other chapters.

If, however, your aim is to gain a thorough grasp of the topic, taking however much time is necessary to do so, you may benefit from carrying out the same procedure with each chapter, as follows:

1 Try to read the chapter in one sitting. As you do this, bear in mind any advice given in the *Points to Consider* section.

2 Study the flow diagram at the end of the chapter, ensuring that you understand the general 'shape' of what you have just read.

3 Read the *Working on . . .* section and decide what further work you need to do on the chapter. In particularly important sections of the book, this is likely to involve reading the chapter a second time and stopping at each heading and sub-heading to think about (and probably to write a summary of) what you have just read.

4 Attempt the *Source-based questions* section. It will sometimes be sufficient to think through your answers, but additional understanding will often be gained by forcing yourself to write them down.

When you have finished the main chapters of the book, study the 'Further Reading' section and decide what additional reading (if any) you will do on the topic.

This book has been designed to help make your studies both enjoyable and successful. If you can think of ways in which this could have been done more effectively, please contact us. In the meantime, we hope that you will gain greatly from your study of History.

Keith Randell & Robert Pearce

1 Introduction: The Irish Question

POINTS TO CONSIDER

The Irish Question was a vitally important, but seemingly insoluble, issue in British politics from the first quarter of the nineteenth century. This chapter introduces you to the nature of the problems posed by Britain's dominance in Ireland and prepares you for the detailed analysis given in later chapters. Your aim should be to grasp the main 'shape' taken by Anglo-Irish affairs in this period.

1 England and Ireland, 1170–1798

KEY ISSUE How and why did Britain come to dominate Ireland?

a) The Conquest of Ireland

The English connection with Ireland began in 1170 when the King of Leinster, wanting military support against his rivals, invited over a group of English knights under the leadership of 'Strongbow' (Richard de Clare). They came for land and wealth, and their military prowess and superior weaponry enabled them to begin the subjugation of the rich, south-eastern part of Ireland, which included important towns such as Dublin and Waterford. Strongbow himself eventually became King of Leinster. The following year King Henry II himself came over to Ireland with a powerful army and pushed forward the conquest of the country. Strongbow, many Irish Gaelic lords and also Church leaders swore allegiance to him. By 1250 about three-quarters of Ireland was under Anglo-Norman control; the main independent area was the province of Ulster, where powerful Gaelic lords, the O'Neills and O'Donnells, still held sway.

During the thirteenth century, as the power of the newcomers advanced, many of the features of Anglo-Norman feudalism were introduced into Ireland. Towns and castles were built; the Norman county and judicial systems were introduced; and Norman notions of personal inheritance and ownership of land were superimposed upon the old Gaelic tradition of family ownership. On the lands that they seized the Anglo-Normans reduced the Irish to the position of serfs. A parliament on the English model was established in 1264, and this represented primarily the power of the new Anglo-Norman ruling class, whose leaders were rewarded with titles.

As the personal control of the English kings over Ireland declined in the later middle ages, due to their involvement in wars abroad and dynastic struggles at home, so the power of the Anglo-Norman lords as a permanent, resident, Irish ruling class grew. Men such as the Earls of Kildare now became almost kings in their own right, giving only a shadowy allegiance to the English Crown. This development was helped by the Anglo-Normans' intermarriage with great Gaelic families, and their partial assimilation of Gaelic customs and culture. By the end of the fifteenth century the English royal government was really only effective in the area round Dublin known as 'the Pale'.

The Tudors, however, with their commitment to a strong, central-ising monarchy as the basis of the state, were determined to re-impose their rule on Ireland. Under Henry VII the task of curbing the pre-tensions of the Irish aristocracy began. His successor went further. In 1541 Henry VIII arranged for the Irish Parliament to declare him King of Ireland, and he followed this up by imposing a new system of land ownership upon the Gaelic lords. He turned the traditional elec-tive Irish lordships into hereditary estates on the English model. This meant that the estates were now held by virtue of the king's law, not by ancient tradition, and that their holders could be dispossessed if they were guilty of disloyalty. In return for submission, prominent Irish lords were rewarded with English titles; the greatest of them, Con O'Neill of Ulster, now became the Earl of Tyrone.

Other problems began when Henry VIII broke with Rome and began the English Reformation. There was much resentment at Henry's anti-papal policy, and the Reformation never really obtained a foothold in Ireland. Henry's anti-papal policy also raised the possi-bility of foreign intervention in Ireland on behalf of the Pope. The prospect of Ireland being used as a backdoor against England was to haunt English rulers and statesmen for centuries to come.

It was Queen Elizabeth I who really carried through the effective conquest of Ireland, and to do this she relied primarily on English commanders and officials. For the queen and many Elizabethans, the English were engaged in a civilising mission in Ireland, and Elizabeth's view of the Irish as 'a rude and barbarous nation' became an assumption of the English governing class for long afterwards. The queen, however, was circumspect in her dealings with Irish Roman Catholicism. Though the major statutes of the Elizabethan church set-tlement applied to Ireland, no real attempt was made to impose Protestantism on the Irish people. Nevertheless, the situation in Ireland was still potentially explosive and there were a number of rebellions against Elizabeth by the Anglo-Norman lords, sometimes in alliance with the Gaelic Irish. The greatest and most dangerous rebel-lion of the reign was that conducted by Hugh O'Neill (Earl of Tyrone) in Ulster in 1595. He was defeated in 1601 at the battle of Kinsale. O'Neill then submitted to the queen and was pardoned, but Ulster was thrown open to English rule. At her death in 1603 Elizabeth could properly claim to have conquered most of Ireland, though English government still hardly impinged upon the lives of the mass of Irish people.

b) The Seventeenth Century

One of the most significant developments in Anglo-Irish history took place in the reign of Elizabeth's successor, James I. This was the 'Plantation of Ulster' in 1610. Tyrone had fled abroad and his lands in western Ulster were seized and opened up to British settlement. But this was just the beginning. The settlement involved the eviction of most of the existing Irish landowners, who were reduced to the status of tenants or labourers for the new landlords, who were mainly Scots. By 1700 Ulster had become mainly a Presbyterian and Anglican province, and the old Catholic ruling class had been displaced. New industry and new towns, including Belfast, began to develop in Ulster; but the 'New English' (as these settlers were known, in contradistinction to the 'Old English', the Anglo-Normans) lived in a state of fear and were hated by the families whose lands they had purloined.

The 1620s and 1630s saw the Gaelic and Old English lords coming closer together in opposition to royal policy, since they had in common both their Roman Catholicism and their opposition to recent land policy. This unity and opposition was increased by the policies pursued by Charles I's representative in Ireland, the Earl of Strafford: greater support for the Anglican Church, more central control and heavier taxation. The removal of Strafford, who was executed by order of the English parliament in 1640, together with the resentments of the Catholic populace at large, culminated in the outbreak of an horrific rebellion in Ulster in 1641. This led to the murder or deaths of several thousand Protestants (and contributed to the Protestants' sense of being a beleaguered minority).The rebels were supported by Catholic forces further south; and by 1648, as a result of the rebellions, alliances and counter-alliances, and general confusion produced by the impact of the Civil War on Ireland, the king's authority was once again confined to the Pale, an area that passed under the control of the English parliament after the final defeat of the royalists.

The execution of King Charles I in 1649 left Oliver Cromwell the most powerful man in the country. For both religious and military reasons Cromwell was now determined to subjugate Ireland. He landed there with a powerful army and, as a contemporary chronicler wrote, 'like lightning passed through the land'. He captured the city of Drogheda in September 1649, and the Catholic garrison was slaughtered in cold blood by the troops of the New Model Army, partly as an act of revenge for the murder of the Ulster Protestants in 1641. A similar policy was applied after the capture of Wexford. For Catholics, Cromwell's ruthlessness has made his name the most execrated in modern Irish history. He abolished the separate Irish parliament, and the Westminster parliament now represented all three kingdoms of England, Ireland and Scotland. He also confiscated about 11 million acres of land, mainly in central Ireland, from those who had supported the king. It was given to his soldiers and supporters. At the time of the Lord Protector's death in 1658, only about one-fifth of all Irish land remained in the hands of Catholics.

In 1660 King Charles II was restored. Yet the Irish gained very little. It is true that Roman Catholics were given practical religious toleration. But Charles II, unwilling to risk his throne by antagonising the Protestant ruling class in England and Ireland, refused to upset the Cromwellian land settlement. The Irish Catholics were therefore forced to accept the loss of their lands. Moreover, though the separate Irish parliament was restored, Catholics were excluded from membership.

James II, crowned in 1685, was an avowed Roman Catholic. Hence the Irish must have hoped for better things. But his pro-Catholic policies soon antagonised the dominant Protestant political classes. The birth of a son, Prince Charles Edward Stuart, raised the possibility of a succession of Roman Catholic monarchs, and as a result leading politicians invited William of Orange (a Dutch Protestant Prince married to James's Protestant daughter, Mary) to invade England and defend the Protestant faith. Thus began the 'Glorious Revolution' of 1688. James fled to France and William and Mary were crowned King and Queen of England. Soon the exiled James went to Ireland, but his effort to regain the throne ended in failure. The lifting of the long siege of Londonderry by William's forces in July 1689 was followed by the defeat of James at the battle of the Boyne in 1690.

c) The Anglican Ascendancy

The downfall of the Catholic cause in Ireland was followed in the eighteenth century by the establishment of the 'Anglican Ascendancy', based on the landownership and the political and religious domination of the members of the Anglican Church of Ireland, which lasted until well into the nineteenth century. The Catholic majority became second-class citizens. Ireland was governed indirectly from England, and the powers of the Irish parliament were severely limited.

Nevertheless, even the Anglican ruling class in Ireland chafed at the restrictions imposed upon them and were not immune from feelings of Irish nationalism. The reformers amongst them, especially 'the Patriots' in the 1750s, demanded more constitutional freedom for the Irish parliament. As a result of that pressure and the impact of the American War of Independence, the government eventually yielded, and by the 'constitution of 1782' the Irish parliament achieved legislative independence. During this same period too, many of the old restrictions on the Catholics in Ireland were lifted.

As so often in history, however, the beginnings of reform whetted the appetite and encouraged the rise of more extreme political movements. In 1791 the Society of United Irishmen was founded by Wolfe

Tone to bring about Irish independence. This could be achieved, Tone believed, by allying with revolutionary France – at war with England after 1793 – and planning a rebellion in Ireland supported by a French invasion.

The rebellion took place in the spring of 1798, but it lacked both leadership and organisation and was quickly defeated by the British army. The surrender of the French invading force in September brought the whole episode to an end. In the eyes of the Prime Minister, William Pitt, the 1798 rebellion revealed all too clearly the weaknesses of the existing, divided system for the government. Plans were put forward for a legislative union between Great Britain and Ireland.

2 Great Britain and the Irish Question

> **KEY ISSUES** What is meant by the 'Irish Question'? How did it change and develop?

a) The Act of Union, 1800

The Act of Union of 1800 abolished the status of Ireland as a separate kingdom and joined her with Great Britain to form the United Kingdom of Great Britain and Ireland (see chapter 2). The separate Irish parliament disappeared, and Ireland was now represented at Westminster. Pitt had intended that union should be followed by Roman Catholic Emancipation (i.e. the granting of full civil and political rights to Roman Catholics, including the right to become MPs). When this did not take place, the Catholics felt betrayed. In Ireland a mass movement developed in the 1820s, led by a young lawyer, Daniel O'Connell, to force the British government to grant their claims. This movement represents the first phase of the 'Irish question', and it lasted until the final passing of the Emancipation Act in 1829.

b) The Emergence of the Irish Question, 1830–50

i) Daniel O'Connell

The passage of the Roman Catholic Emancipation Act of 1829 proved to be the most significant achievement of Daniel O'Connell as an Irish nationalist leader (see chapter 3). The Act gave Roman Catholics full civil and political rights, with a few minor exceptions; and since they could now become MPs, it was followed by the emergence of a small Irish Party in the House of Commons. The early 1830s therefore mark the real beginning of the 'Irish question' as an important feature of British political life.

What, then, was meant by the 'Irish question'? At its heart, according to English politicians, was the unreasonable refusal of the Irish majority to acknowledge the obvious benefits which Union was bringing. After all, the Roman Catholics from 1829 onwards were in possession of full civil and political rights: they could become MPs, hold public office and participate fully in British political life. They also had security against invasion as a result of British power; they benefited economically by being associated with British capital, commerce and industry; and they were now party to a more advanced, progressive civilisation, which was also the centre of a world-wide Empire.

Yet such arguments cut little ice with the Irish, particularly the more nationalist-minded among them. For many Irish Catholics the 'golden age' lay in the past – in the great period of Irish Christianity between the seventh and the ninth centuries A.D. Nor did they regard the increasingly materialistic civilisation of contemporary England as something to be admired. They sensed the contempt for Irish religion and culture which lay behind English views. Moreover, as rapid population growth pressed ever harder on Irish resources, the supposed economic benefits of the Union seemed more and more illusory. In any case, as nationalist leaders argued, the Act of Union had been imposed upon them and produced subordination, not equality, for Ireland. The Union, in the words of one Irish nationalist, was 'a nullity, a usurpation and a fraud'.

The conclusion drawn from all this by O'Connell was his declaration in 1842: 'I want every Irishman to be convinced of this truth, that there is nothing worth looking for, save the power of governing ourselves'. After 1840 he organised a new campaign – modelled on the successful movement for Roman Catholic emancipation – which aimed at the repeal of the Union. The Repeal campaign of the early 1840s forms the second major phase in O'Connell's career as an Irish nationalist leader.

Movements such as this forced Englishmen to accept the reality of Irish opposition to the Union – though admittedly this was often attributed to the irrationality of the Irish character or the intimidation of the Irish masses by a minority of extremists. In a rather perplexed way, it was gradually accepted that Ireland was a special area within the United Kingdom and demanded special treatment. Nevertheless, every major English politician was convinced that for the good of all, including the Irish people, the Union must be maintained. The most difficult aspect of the Irish question that emerged, therefore, after 1830, was: how was loyalty to the Union to be maintained in the teeth of Irish opposition? The answer given by all parties was that the Irish majority must be won over by policies which improved and modernised Irish society and provided the framework for future peace and prosperity. At the same time special, extra-legal measures could be imposed to stamp out violent opposition. This dual programme (reform and coercion) was pursued by all British governments until the Act of Union was ended in 1921–2.

The first period of Irish reform came from the Whigs in the 1830s and Sir Robert Peel and the Conservatives in the 1840s (see chapter 3) – mainly adminstrative measure dealing with education, the poor law, and local government. Nothing was done yet to tackle the major grievances of the Irish over religion, land and government. Disraeli's classic description of the problem in 1844 therefore still applied: 'Thus you have a starving population, an absentee aristocracy, and an alien Church, and in addition the weakest executive in the world. That is the Irish question'.

At the same time as Peel strove to placate the Irish through a programme of reform, he also curbed the Repeal campaign itself in 1843–4, and the movement declined and eventually collapsed after O'Connell's death in 1847.

ii) The Great Famine
One reason for the difficulties faced by O'Connell in the later 1840s was the onset of the Great Famine (1845–9) which, as a result of the failure of the potato crop, led to starvation, disease and death on a large scale in Ireland. It forms a major landmark in the history of modern Ireland. Peel tried to prevent mass starvation through the repeal of the Corn Laws in the summer of 1846, while his successor, Lord John Russell, carried through a variety of relief measures (see chapter 4) down to 1849. The consequences of the famine are of enormous importance for Ireland and, indirectly, for the history of the Irish question in Great Britain.

c) Gladstone and Ireland
Comparative political tranquillity descended on Ireland in the wake of the Great Famine, and the Irish question receded into the background of British politics in the mid-nineteenth century. It re-emerged, however, when the Liberal leader, W.E. Gladstone, outlined a new programme of Irish reform after his great victory at the polls in the general election of 1868. Gladstone dominated the history of the Irish question from 1868 until the failure of his Second Home Rule Bill in 1893 (see chapters 5 and 6).

Whatever Gladstone's motives for taking up the Irish question, his major aim was exactly the same as that of his Whig and Tory predecessors: to build up support for the Union in Ireland by remedying outstanding Irish grievances. Indeed John Vincent controversially describes Gladstone as 'the most masterly upholder of Unionism since Pitt'. The two problems he was particularly concerned with were religion, notably the position of the minority Anglican Church as the Established Church of Ireland, and land, more especially landlord-tenant relations. The emergence of these two issues had important consequences for the development of the Irish question in British politics. For whereas earlier Irish reforms were on the whole acceptable to members of all parties, this was not true of Gladstone's. The Conservative Party – traditionally the party of the Church of England – believed that the idea of disestablishing the Church of Ireland would (in the contemporary phrase) 'cross the water' and lead to demands for the disestablishment of the Church of England. Similarly, interference with the property rights of landlords in Ireland might encourage attacks on landlords' rights in England. The Irish question after 1868 thus became an important issue dividing the Liberals and Conservatives.

The Irish Church Act of 1869 disestablished and disendowed the Anglican Church in Ireland, thus destroying its privileged status and taking over its property. As a result, the religious problem in Ireland was more or less solved. Yet Gladstone's two Irish Land Acts of 1870 and 1881, which limited landlords' rights over their tenants, did little to solve the fundamental problems of the Irish rural economy. Nor did Gladstone's legislation as a whole achieve the major political result – namely, Irish support for the Union – for which he had hoped. This was partly because of the emergence of the Irish Land League and the rise of Charles Stewart Parnell as the leader of the Irish Home Rule Party (see chapters 5 and 6).

By the end of 1885 Gladstone was convinced that his programme of reform had failed. Only Home Rule – that is, a measure of self-government for Ireland – would, he believed, now suffice. He was convinced of this by the growing support for the Home Rule Party in Ireland, as shown by the general election in November of that year. Yet both of his Home Rule Bills failed. In 1886 the First Home Rule Bill was rejected by the House of Commons, mainly because of a revolt by an important section of the Liberal Party. In 1893 the Second Home Rule Bill was passed by the Commons but rejected by a massive majority in the House of Lords.

Gladstone retired as Liberal leader in 1894, and in the general election the following year his party suffered an overwhelming defeat. The Liberals remained out of power until 1905. They won a landslide victory in 1906, but it was not until 1911 that Home Rule re-emerged as an important, practical issue.

d) The Ulster Problem

Why did Asquith's Liberal government take up again the thorny problem of Home Rule which had twice defeated Gladstone? Their motives are much disputed among historians (see chapter 7). All agree, however, on the vital link between the Parliament Act of 1911 and the cause of Home Rule. The 1911 Act meant that a bill passed by the Commons could only be held up by the Lords for a maximum of two years, and therefore for the first time a Home Rule Bill could eventually become law despite its rejection by the Upper House. In this new context, the Irish question came to dominate British politics in the years before the outbreak of the First World War.

Asquith's Home Rule Bill, presented to the Commons in April 1912, was a moderate measure, similar in most respects to Gladstone's 1893 Bill. In particular, like that measure, it provided for Home Rule for all Ireland. But in the intervening period the divisions between Catholics and Protestants in Ireland had hardened, and the Liberals now found themselves faced by the united, stubborn resistance of the Ulster unionists. In opposing the Liberals' policy over Ireland the Ulstermen were backed up by the Conservative Party in England, which was prepared to use Ulster extremism to destroy the new Home Rule Bill – and, they hoped, the Liberal government.

The crisis mounted. Though compromise solutions were suggested – based on the possibility of 'excluding' the distinctly Protestant counties of Ulster from the operation of Home Rule – no agreement had been reached by the time Great Britain entered the First World War on 4 August 1914.

e) The Making of the Anglo-Irish Settlement of 1920–2

The war had a profound effect on the development of the Irish question. In Ireland itself it encouraged the supersession of the parliamentary Irish Nationalist Party by the more militant organisation of Sinn Fein ('Ourselves Alone'), which was committed to complete independence and the establishment of an Irish Republic. The war also helped to give the Irish question an international dimension: the influence of the United States (with its large and influential Irish-American community) was boosted, while Allied statesmen at the Paris Peace Conference in 1919 voiced a commitment to national self-determination.

Even while the war was still on, attempts were made by the Coalition governments of Asquith and, later, Lloyd George, to obtain agreement between the Irish Nationalists and Unionists, both of whom supported the war, on an immediate political settlement based on the principle of Home Rule plus 'exclusion'. All failed. In any case, the growing unpopularity of the war in southern Ireland, together with the powerful influence of the Easter Rebellion of 1916 in arousing Irish national consciousness and anti-British feeling, meant that Home Rule was no longer a viable solution to the Irish question. This was revealed dramatically in the general election of 1918 that followed the November Armistice: Sinn Fein won almost every seat in southern Ireland (see chapter 8).

Sinn Fein leaders, now claiming to be the rightful representatives of the Irish people, demanded an English withdrawal. It set up its own parliament in Dublin and proclaimed the establishment of the Irish Republic. Since the British government had no intention of aban-

A map of the counties of Ireland

doning its sovereignty over Ireland, these demands led inexorably to the outbreak of a vicious war between the two sides.

In 1920 the British government made one more attempt to produce an acceptable political settlement. The Government of Ireland Act of that year was based on the principle of Home Rule for both parts of Ireland: local parliaments and representative governments were to be set up for both Northern Ireland (consisting of the six most Protestant counties) and Southern Ireland (26 counties). In the north, an Ulster Unionist government soon came into power; but in the south the Act was completely ignored by Sinn Fein, whose leaders insisted on nothing less than full independence for the whole of Ireland. Once again British views on Ireland were far behind the tempo of events. The Anglo-Irish war therefore continued.

By the spring of 1921, however, both the British government and the Irish republican leadership were war-weary. A truce was agreed to in July. It was followed by long-drawn-out negotiations between an Irish delegation and a small ministerial team headed by Lloyd George, which led eventually to the signing of an Anglo-Irish Treaty in December 1921. It was ratified the following year. This brought an end to the war. Politically, it led to the establishment of a virtually independent Irish Free State of 26 counties, though the existence of the state of Northern Ireland as a *fait accompli* was also recognised (see the map on page 10).

3 Historians and the Irish Question

> **KEY ISSUE** What are the main ways in which historians have interpreted the Irish question?

To some extent historians' outlooks on the Irish question have been determined by their nationality. England's dominance over Ireland meant that, inevitably, Ireland had little direct impact on the development of her more powerful neighbour. For English historians, therefore, the Anglo-Irish relationship has formed only a minor part of modern English history. Even when the Irish question has impinged more directly on England, as during the Home Rule crises and the Anglo-Irish war, the attitude of English historians has on the whole been Anglocentric: Irish affairs are looked at through English eyes and with English concerns in mind. *The Governing Passion: Cabinet Government and Party Politics in Britain 1885–86* (1974), by A.B. Cooke and John Vincent, and Patricia Jalland's *The Liberals and Ireland: the Ulster Question in British Politics to 1914* (1980), are outstanding examples of this approach. Both books have been criticised in some respects by other scholars, but it cannot be said that the study of

Anglo-Irish relations has aroused any great passions among English professional historians.

None of this is true for Irish historians. For Irish nationalist historians – the dominant group in Irish historical writing up to about the 1960s – the very shape and substance of modern Irish history has been determined by the forced connection with England. For these historians, Irish history since the later eighteenth century is the story of a united people – conscious of their separate national identity and inspired by a long line of outstanding nationalist leaders – joining together to oppose the tyranny of England and, in the end, compelling her to retreat and abandon most of Ireland. The fulfilment of that story, with a united Ireland, must eventually come. Thus, as P.S. O'Hegarty writes in his *A History of Ireland under the Union* (Dublin, 1952), Irish history is 'the story of a people coming out of captivity . . . finding every artery of national life occupied by the enemy, recovering them one by one, and coming out at last into the full blaze of the sun'.

For nationalist historians then, Irish history since 1800 has a pattern and a purpose: historical development proceeds along a fixed line to a pre-determined end. Yet such nationalist history is too simple. It highlights the role of nationalist heroes and martyrs, often inspired by the Catholic faith, as the embodiment of the will of the Irish people; and it provides a 'mythical' interpretation of key events, based on their emotional appeal – the 1798 rebellion and the Easter Rebellion of 1916, for example – to sustain that nationalist fervour. This sort of history reads the past through the eyes of the present, and its purpose is to raise Irish nationalist consciousness and justify the revolutionary tradition.

Since roughly the 1960s, so-called 'revisionists' have come to the fore, in deliberate opposition to the nationalist tradition. They have a far less committed view of Irish history and the Anglo-Irish relationship. The revisionists see no special pattern or purpose in Irish history, and nor do they regard the English connection as the only factor that explains Irish development. As historians, they serve no particular cause and have no public mission other than the desire to use the established techniques of the professional historian to achieve the 'truth' about the past.

The revisionists have therefore tried to penetrate behind the myths and simplifications of the nationalist historians to the detailed, often complicated, context in which historical events actually occur. This has often led them to discern disunity and conflict in many aspects of Irish history, where the nationalists see only unity and continuity. In particular – to the fury of many – they have sounded a more sceptical note in discussing the ideals and methods of modern Irish nationalism, and have insisted on giving full weight to the reality of Ulster unionism. They have also laid a new stress on the importance of social and economic history. Much of the recent work on landownership in

Ireland, for example – which has exploded many myths about the conditions of landlords and tenants and the results of land reform – has been due to their inspiration. One result of this detailed work has been to render suspect the traditional view that all Ireland's economic ills can be blamed on England. Indeed, revisionist history has shown that at particular periods economic prosperity was a reality for some groups in Irish Catholic society. All these issues are discussed at length in Roy Foster's outstanding revisionist history, *Modern Ireland 1600–1972* (1988).

The revisionists have now been fiercely attacked by a number of younger Irish historians sympathetic to nationalist aspirations. It has been argued that revisionist history lacks 'empathy and imagination'; it plays down what has been called (by Dr Brendan Bradshaw, its major critic) 'the catastrophic dimension' in Irish history, especially in relation to the Great Famine. Revisionist history is thus out of touch, it is suggested, with the deepest feelings of the Irish majority. Bradshaw is critical of the false 'objectivity' of the revisionists and castigates them for retreating to an ivory tower. Yet Bradshaw has in turn been criticised by one senior historian for abandoning 'the status of history as a detached scholarly activity'. And so the debate continues.

Working on Chapter 1

Detailed notes are not required. But try to keep the main pattern of Anglo-Irish affairs in mind as you read the succeeding chapters. In this way you will see specific events in a wider context.

Summary Diagram

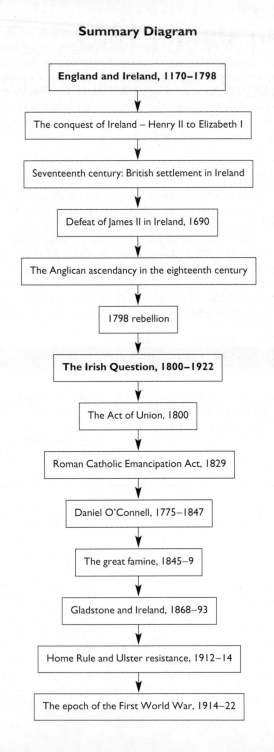

England and Ireland, 1170–1798

↓

The conquest of Ireland – Henry II to Elizabeth I

↓

Seventeenth century: British settlement in Ireland

↓

Defeat of James II in Ireland, 1690

↓

The Anglican ascendancy in the eighteenth century

↓

1798 rebellion

↓

The Irish Question, 1800–1922

↓

The Act of Union, 1800

↓

Roman Catholic Emancipation Act, 1829

↓

Daniel O'Connell, 1775–1847

↓

The great famine, 1845–9

↓

Gladstone and Ireland, 1868–93

↓

Home Rule and Ulster resistance, 1912–14

↓

The epoch of the First World War, 1914–22

2 The Making of the Act of Union, 1800

POINTS TO CONSIDER

The focus of this chapter is the Act of Union, which its supporters hoped would improve Anglo-Irish relations but which in fact did the opposite. Yet the Act, though important for what followed, was itself part of a broad historical process. Hence you should be sure not to neglect the sections in this chapter covering the period before 1800, where many of the fundamental issues are identified.

KEY DATES

1750s	the Patriots were formed
1760	formation of the Catholic Committee
1779–80	free trade for Ireland
1782	constitutional reform in Ireland
1791	Society of United Irishmen formed
1795	Orange Order in Ulster
1798	(May–December) Irish Rebellion
1800	Act of Union passed

1 The Ascendancy in Eighteenth-Century Ireland

> **KEY ISSUE** In what ways was Ireland subordinate to England before 1800?

The defeat of James II at the battle of the Boyne in 1690 ensured the triumph of Protestantism and the defeat of Catholicism in England and Ireland, a supremacy confirmed by the accession of the Protestant Elector of Hanover as King George I in 1714 and the subsequent defeat of the Jacobite rebellions of 1715 and 1745. As a result, penal laws were passed against Catholics after 1689: they could not vote, sit in parliament or hold any public office. In addition – in an age when land and political power went hand in hand – Irish Catholics were also limited in their right to purchase or inherit land, and forbidden to bear arms. They did in practice possess religious toleration, but the penal code impeded their right to a Catholic education and forced a number of their clergy to emigrate. Some of these penal laws applied also to the Irish Dissenters, including the powerful Presbyterian community of Ulster. Although they possessed freedom of religion and could generally vote, as non-Anglicans they were denied the right to hold public office.

All this paved the way for the emergence of what became known as the 'Ascendancy' in eighteenth-century Ireland. The Anglican social elite dominated Irish politics, society and the economy. Their power stemmed from ownership of the bulk of the land. By the mid-eighteenth century Catholics owned only about five per cent of the land, at a time when they formed about 75 per cent of the population. A small class of Catholic gentry did survive, mainly in the west, but the majority of Catholics now existed as small tenant farmers, renting land from their Protestant landlords, or as landless labourers living in conditions of appalling squalor and poverty.

The other pillar of the Ascendancy was of course the Anglican Church of Ireland. Since by law it was the Established Church – even though it represented only about 15 per cent of the people of Ireland – it possessed wealth, privileges and influence. It had, for example, representatives sitting in the Irish House of Lords, and possessed the right to collect tithes from the whole population – something which aroused bitter resentment among Catholics and Presbyterians alike. Not surprisingly, the Church of Ireland was regarded as a major instrument in the English control of Ireland.

Unlike its Scottish neighbour which by the Act of Union of 1707 had joined with England to form the Kingdom of Great Britain, Ireland remained a separate and dependent kingdom, as it had been since the reign of Henry VIII. In a number of ways Ireland's status was akin to that of a colony. Administration was controlled by the Lord-Lieutenant (or Viceroy), the British government's representative in Ireland, who was generally a scion of the English aristocracy and a member of the Cabinet. Below the Lord-Lieutenant were the various ministers and officials, many of them Englishmen, who were responsible for the day-to-day running of the Irish government and were known collectively as 'the Castle', since Dublin Castle was the Viceroy's official residence. The Chief Secretary was responsible for getting the government's legislation through the Irish parliament. This was a major task which could only be accomplished successfully by building up support among its members through the lavish distribution of titles and lucrative offices controlled by the government.

Although the Irish parliament had existed since the thirteenth century and was modelled on that of England, its powers were severely limited. By Poyning's Law of 1494 and the later Declaratory Act of 1719, Ireland was subject to the laws of the Westminster parliament, and its own parliament could only pass laws ultimately approved by the British government. Thus the Irish parliament lacked any real legislative initiative, and, since the Lord-Lieutenant was the nominee of the British government, the Irish legislature had no control over its own Executive. Moreover, the Irish parliament only met when summoned by the Crown. The Septennial Act of 1715 (which provided for general elections at least every seven years) did not apply to Ireland.

Nevertheless, despite its weaknesses, the Irish parliament was not always amenable to government direction. This was particularly so when questions involving finance or Irish economic interests were involved and the parliament could rely on the backing of public opinion. In 1725, for example, the government was forced to withdraw a new Irish coinage manufactured in England ('Wood's Ha'pence') because of public pressure. As a result of this affair, suggests one historian, 'Protestant nationalism was born'.

2 The Age of Revolution

> **KEY ISSUE** For what reasons, and with what results, did a rebellion break out in 1798?

In the later eighteenth century Protestant nationalism steadily advanced in Ireland. There was a growing feeling in the Protestant communities that, although they were divided by race and religion from the majority of Irish people, they too were Irish by nationality and should put the interests of Ireland first. This conviction led in the 1750s to the emergence in the Irish House of Commons of the minority group of MPs known as the 'Patriots', whose most notable leader was Henry Grattan. His leadership was a result of his personality, his powers of oratory and his devotion to the cause. The Patriots denounced the subordination of Ireland to Great Britain. They demanded commercial equality for Ireland and legislative independence for the Irish parliament, to be accompanied by regular elections and an attack on the corruption of the Castle's rule. Nor were the Catholics unaffected by these developments. The formation of the Catholic Committee in 1760 as a moderate, constitutional organisation for the redress of Catholic grievances is a reflection of this. As Grattan said: 'the Irish Protestant can never be free, till the Irish Catholic had ceased to be a slave'. Something of an unofficial alliance was therefore built up during this period between the moderate reformers in both communities.

In the 1760s the British government was prepared to make some concessions. For instance, it was conceded that the Lord-Lieutenant should be permanently resident in Ireland, and the process of reforming the patronage system was begun. In addition, an Octennnial Act was passed in 1768, so that general elections had to be held at least every eight years. However, it was the outbreaks of the American War of Independence in 1775 and of the French Revolution in 1789 which did most to encourage the process of reform, and which profoundly affected the relationship between Great Britain and Ireland.

a) The American War

Whereas the Catholics in Ireland remained loyal to the Crown during the War of American Independence (1775–82), and thereby won some minor improvements in the penal code, the Protestants were more sympathetic to the colonists. They too saw themselves as suffering from subordination to the parliament in Westminster. The Ulster Presbyterians, in particular, had strong links with America through emigration, and the political ideas of the American rebels, exemplified by their slogan 'No Taxation without Representation', appealed to their own radical outlook. 'We are all Americans here', wrote one Patriot, 'except such as are attached to the Castle or are papists'.

The influence of the Patriots was boosted by the support of the Volunteer movement, which sprang up spontaneously in 1778 and numbered 30–40,000 members two years later. The Volunteers were pledged to repel any foreign invader, but they undoubtedly represented the military arm of Protestant nationalism. Their strong support for the political programme of the Patriots is shown by one of their marching songs:

> No laws shall ever bind but those we frame ourselves.
> The Britons now shall find us as free as they're themselves.
> Hibernia's Volunteers, boys, have worked the glorious cause
> And will with mighty heart and head abolish Poyning's Laws.

Lord North recognised the power wielded by the Volunteer and Patriot alliance in favour of reform. His government yielded to the economic demands of the Irish opposition, so that in 1779–80 most of the restrictions on Irish commerce were abolished and 'free trade for Ireland' was introduced. Greater change occurred, however, when North resigned after the British surrender to the rebels at Yorktown in 1782. He was replaced by Lord Rockingham and the Whigs, who for years had been strong supporters of the Patriots' cause. By the 'constitution of 1782', which the Whigs now introduced, Poyning's Law and the Declaratory Act of 1719 were repealed, and the Irish parliament for the first time in its history achieved legislative independence. This meant that though the Crown retained a final veto over legislation, the initiative belonged to the Irish House of Commons, which could pass its own laws without the consent of the government in Great Britain. In this way 'Grattan's Parliament', as it is always known – in tribute to its greatest member – began its short life. 'Ireland is now a nation', he proclaimed. 'In that new character I hail her.'

Yet despite Grattan's euphoria, the changes were more apparent than real. Ireland's parliament still had no control over the Executive, and the Lord-Lieutenants could still contrive, though with greater difficulty than previously, to control the Commons' proceedings through the time-honoured methods of influence, patronage and electoral corruption. All this meant that the major demand of the reformers (as with their fellow-radicals in England) now became parliamentary reform, aimed at making the Irish parliament truly representative of the people. For Patriots like Grattan this implied political rights for Catholics too, something which the Catholic Committee itself had been vigorously demanding. Yet this was an issue over which the Ascendancy itself was divided, and in the later 1780s parliament rejected any attempt to liberalise the 'Constitution of 1782'. Nor could the reformers now expect much sympathy at Westminster. The accession of the Younger Pitt to office as Prime Minister in 1783 began a long period of strong and stable government in defence of the political and social status quo.

There were also growing economic and social problems in Ireland. Although these years saw a considerable increase in the prosperity of the Irish middle classes, especially in Ulster, owing to the expansion of trade, the rapid increase in Irish population throughout the eighteenth century exacerbated the competition for land and helped to produce sporadic outbreaks of violence. All these problems were to come to a head during the period of the French Revolution.

b) The Impact of the French Revolution

The outbreak of the French Revolution stimulated the demand for further reform throughout Ireland, especially in Ulster where the Volunteer movement, though in decline elsewhere, remained powerful. Even the Catholic Committee became more radical. It was the need to conciliate the Catholics, especially after the outbreak of war with France in 1793, and fears of a Catholic-Presbyterian anti-government alliance, that led Pitt to force further reforms on a reluctant Viceroy and parliament. In 1793 Catholics were granted the right to vote, and most civil and military posts in Ireland were thrown open to them. In this way a young Catholic lawyer, Daniel O'Connell – the future 'Liberator' (see page 37) – became a member of the Irish Bar.

These concessions did little to improve the status of the Irish Catholics since they were still denied the right to sit in parliament or to hold public office, and the old pattern of Anglican-dominated politics remained. Hence the era of the French Revolution placed the demand for Roman Catholic emancipation firmly on the political agenda of the opposition both in Ireland and England, and this question was inextricably linked with the wider aim of parliamentary reform.

The government's obstinate refusal to shift its position on either the 'emancipation' or the 'parliamentary reform' question during this period not only helped to push Catholic and Protestant radicals closer together, but also inevitably encouraged the growth of more extreme reform movements. The 1790s therefore saw the emergence of a new, and ultimately more militant, organisation, the Society of United Irishmen, led by a young Protestant lawyer, Wolfe Tone.

c) The Society of United Irishmen

The Society of United Irishmen was originally formed in 1791 as an organisation of radical clubs in Ulster. Its aim was to influence Irish opinion in favour of the twin aims of Catholic emancipation and parliamentary reform. In the years that followed, particularly as a result of the increasingly reactionary attitudes of the Irish government and parliament, and the developing revolutionary fervour of Wolfe Tone, the society transformed itself into a more secretive, extremist and quasi-military organisation. It now appealed deliberately to all Irishmen and aimed at the establishment of an independent Irish republic. By 1797 the Society was believed to possess more than 100,000 active supporters.

Wolfe Tone became more intensely anti-British and pro-French, and since Britain and France were now at war, the idea of military help from France as the only means of salvation for Ireland, became more and more appealing. 'To subvert the tyranny of our execrable government', he wrote, 'to break the connection with England, the never-failing source of all our political evils, and to assert the independence of my country – these are my objects'. The notion of liberation from British rule was bound to have an appeal, not just to middle-class radicals, but also to the Catholic peasantry, who had their own economic grievances against the Protestant landlord and the Anglican Church. This led to fierce outbreaks of sectarian strife in the north. In response, a number of Ulster Protestants combined together in 1795 to form the loyalist Orange Order, based largely on the former Volunteers, to defend Protestantism and the British Crown – a task it has been committed to ever since. Some Catholics therefore turned to the Society of United Irishmen to defend them against this Protestant backlash.

By this time the British government, alarmed at the growth of subversive ideas in the middle of a major war, was preparing to move against the Irish radicals. Wolfe Tone therefore fled to America in 1795 and from there he made his way to Paris, where he began plotting with the French authorities for an invasion of Ireland. A fleet did set sail at the end of 1796 and reached Bantry Bay, but owing to a storm it was forced to withdraw.

Action had already been taken by the British to stamp out the radical opposition. Earlier in 1796 magistrates in Ireland had been given wider powers to seize arms and arrest suspects. Even more provocatively, a force of loyalist Protestant yeomanry had been set up to act on behalf of the government. Now, in 1797, a mainly yeomanry force under the command of General Lake moved against the United Irishmen in Belfast determined to destroy their leadership and their support. 'Our aim', said one officer, 'was to excite terror and by that means obtain our end speedily'. To a large extent their brutal campaign of repression succeeded; and the following year the yeomanry moved against the United Irishmen in the south, especially in Dublin. Martial law was proclaimed. It was in these circumstances, that the rump of the United Irishmen, largely leaderless and with their organisation in disarray, decided that their only hope now was through rebellion coupled with a French invasion.

d) The Rebellion of 1798

The disintegration of the Society of United Irishmen meant that it was unable to impose its grip on the long-awaited rebellion which broke out in Ireland on 23 May 1798. The rebellion therefore consisted of a series of separate uprisings, based primarily on local grievances rather than any overriding set of ideas or concerted plan. At the time, some members of the Ascendancy saw it as basically a Catholic rebellion against Protestantism. But Lord Cornwallis, the Viceroy, denounced 'the folly of substituting Catholic instead of Jacobin as the foundation of the present rebellion', and a fellow member of the government similarly argued that it was due to 'French policies and French success ... [and] the jargon of equality'.

In fact it was only among a minority in Ulster that French revolutionary ideas were important, and the rebellion there, as in the west of Ireland, was a limited affair. The main area where the outbreak was bitter and protracted was in the south-east, especially in Wexford, and there it did take the form of something like a bloody religious war. Groups of Protestants were massacred by Catholic insurgents, and the yeomanry responded in kind, sometimes resorting to a 'scorched earth' policy against Catholic property.

But, given the strength and determination of the government forces, the rebellion had no real chance of success, and after General Lake's victory at Vinegar Hill on 21 June, it rapidly petered out. The captured rebel leaders were executed or suffered transportation, but the rank-and-file were allowed to return to their homes. Although the rebellion lasted barely a month, it has been estimated that by the end of that summer the death toll on both sides amounted to about 30,000. It has been suggested that 'The 1798 rising was probably the most concentrated episode of violence in Irish history'.

The fact that it was only in August, after the rebellion was more or less over, that the French made their invasion attempt ensured that it was virtually a doomed enterprise from the start. The French landed in County Mayo in the west with barely a thousand men and were forced to surrender early in September. By that time another French expedition, including Wolfe Tone, had set sail for Ireland, but it was scattered by a British naval force and most of the French ships were captured. Tone was one of the prisoners taken. He was condemned to death as a rebel but cheated the hangman's noose by committing suicide. He was only 35.

In this way the hoped-for 'Year of Liberation' ended with the apparent triumph of the forces of reaction. But things were never to be the same again. In the long run the life and death of Wolfe Tone and the history of the Society of United Irishmen became part of the mythology of Irish republican nationalism, which adopted the society's colour – green – as its symbol. More immediately, the demand for fundamental constitutional change was gaining ground. Even before the rebellion there were fears by members of the governing class both in Britain and Ireland that, as a result of the disagreements arising out of the constitution of 1782, the two countries would drift further and further apart. This was bound to imperil the security of both. The fears and doubts inspired by the events of 1798 meant, therefore, that the arguments in favour of a union of the two kingdoms became more powerful and imperative to the British government and its supporters on both sides of the Irish sea.

3 The Act of Union, 1800

> **KEY ISSUES** What hopes were entertained for the Act of Union and how far were these fulfilled?

Even before the end of the Irish rebellion William Pitt had begun to consider the possibility of a union between the two kingdoms of Great Britain and Ireland, coupled with Catholic emancipation. 'The idea of the present fermentation', the Prime Minister wrote, 'gradually bringing both parties to think of a union with this country had long been in my mind. The admission of the Catholics to a share of suffrage would not then be dangerous'. Although Pitt obtained strong support within the British and Irish governments, he was forced in the end to abandon the plan for combining union with emancipation owing to the opposition of important and influential members of the Ascendancy. He decided, therefore, initially to concentrate on obtaining the support of the Irish parliament for the principle of union. Catholic emancipation could be worked for once union had been achieved.

The Irish parliament considered the issue of union at the end of January 1799 in a series of highly charged debates held amid intense public interest and excitement in Dublin. In the end the government proposal was narrowly defeated. But Pitt remained determined to get an Act of Union passed. He paved the way for legislation by dismissing ministers and officials opposed to union, and he then gave

Viscount Castlereagh, the Chief Secretary, the task of winning over Irish public opinion. In the course of the next year both unionist and anti-unionist forces attempted to build up support for their respective causes. Most Irishmen, inevitably concerned with the hardships of their daily lives, were probably unconcerned, and the politically concerned minority were profoundly divided. Some groups found it difficult to decide and just awaited events. What then were the arguments for and against union?

a) Arguments For

Pro-unionists stressed the hard facts of geography and military power. At the moment Ireland was the weak link in the system of imperial defence: union, however, would enable the British government to assume direct responsibility for the defence of Ireland against rebellion and foreign invasion. Furthermore, the present system of government divided between London and Dublin, together with a separate and now independent Irish parliament, only encouraged divisions, acrimony and inefficiency – weaknesses which could be fatal in the middle of a great war. Besides, the fate of the Ascendancy itself was at stake. Its very existence had always rested ultimately on the military power of Great Britain: union would make palpable this simple but inescapable fact. As Lord Clare, the Lord Chancellor, argued to his fellow members of the Irish parliament with brutal clarity:

1 From their first settlement they [the English settlers] have been hemmed in on every side by the old inhabitants of this island, brooding over their discontents in sullen indignation. What was the security of the English settlers for their physical existence? And what is the secur-
5 ity of their descendants at this day? The powerful and commanding position of Great Britain. If, by any fatality it fails, you are at the mercy of the old inhabitants of this island.

William Pitt preferred to stress the more positive benefits of union, especially in the economic field. Union would enable Ireland to become part of the wider British economy, and, as the Scottish Union had shown, this would produce clear advantages for the Irish people, especially by encouraging economic growth and prosperity. Moreover, the fact that the Roman Catholics would only be a minority within a United Kingdom (whereas they were the overwhelming majority in Ireland itself) would remove the traditional fears of Protestants, and would make them more prepared to grant equal rights to their Catholic fellow-citizens. As Castlereagh said, 'strength and confidence will encourage liberality'. In a wider sense too, the hatreds of Irish life would be tempered by 'a moral assimilation' (in the phrase of an Anglican cleric) into British society, and this would undermine the age-old differences between the Irish Celt and the Anglo-Saxon, and thus sustain the union.

As Pitt explained to the British House of Commons in January 1799 in supporting the idea of union:

1 What are the positive advantages that Ireland is to derive from it? ... the protection which she will secure to herself in the hour of danger, the most effectual means of increasing her commerce and improving her agriculture, the command of English capital, the infusion of English
5 manners and English industry, necessarily tending to ameliorate her condition ... and to terminate those feuds and dissensions which now distract the country, and which she does not possess, within herself, the power either to control or extinguish ... But ... the question is not only what Ireland is to gain, but what she is to preserve ... In this view, what
10 she gains is the preservation of all those blessings arising from the British constitution, and which are inseparable from her connection with Great Britain.

b) Arguments Against

The arguments of the opponents of union were more emotional, and were based primarily on a vague feeling of Irish nationality. They insisted that Ireland was a separate society with its own distinctive institutions and interests, and should therefore possess its own independent parliament, even though it bore allegiance to the British Crown. The record of that parliament, based on the constitution of 1782, had clearly justified its existence. Ireland was now a more prosperous and cultivated society, the arts flourished, and Dublin was a major European city. 'God and nature', affirmed one anti-unionist MP, 'never intended Ireland to be a province, and by God she never shall'.

It was, argued the opponents of union, the Ascendancy which had helped Ireland to make so much progress in the eighteenth century, and it was the Ascendancy which had crushed the rebellion of 1798. 'How was the rebellion put down?' asked another like-minded MP. 'By the zeal and loyalty of the gentlemen of Ireland rallying round the laws, the constitution and the independence of their country'. Destroy that independence, and Ireland would once again be under the heel of Great Britain and decline into a provincial backwater. As Sir John Foster, the Attorney-General, one of the major parliamentary opponents of union, argued:

1 Can those who hear me now deny that since the period of 1782 this country has risen in civilisation, wealth and manufactures, until interrupted by the present war, much more than it ever did itself in a like period before? And what has this improvement been owing to but the
5 spirit, the content and enterprise which a free Constitution inspired? ... I admit that this kingdom is dependent on the Crown of Great Britain ... but it is dependent only on the Crown ... whereas if we adopt the proposed Union ... we shall be brought back to the miserable state in

which we were when governed by the laws of another parliament sit-
10 ting in another land, ruled by their will, not by our own.

Perhaps the opponents of union protested too much. For their arguments possessed one fatal flaw: the 'nation' they claimed to speak for – like the Irish parliament itself – represented only a tiny minority of the Irish people. The Catholics still remained outside the political nation. By and large the Ascendancy had continued to set its face against both Catholic emancipation and parliamentary reform. After the events of 1798 all it wished to do was to return to the status quo – back to the very situation which had brought it to the verge of disaster. 'The noble lord calls upon us for an alternative', said one leading anti-unionist MP, addressing Lord Castlereagh, 'we want no alternative – we call for a sacred adherence to the constitution of 1782'. Admittedly some anti-unionists, like Henry Grattan, did support both Catholic emancipation and parliamentary reform, but that stance merely revealed the divisions within the anti-unionist camp. All this made it difficult for them to make an effective stand against the attacks of their opponents. Ireland in 1799, in the harsh phrase of one historian, was 'politically bankrupt'.

c) The Passage of the Act

During the months that followed Pitt's initial failure, events appeared to move in favour of the government. Since, as we have seen, the anti-unionists seemed to have nothing positive to offer, leading members of the Roman Catholic clergy and laity came out in support of union, encouraged by the belief that Catholic emancipation would follow. Fears of French invasion resurfaced in 1799–1800, and this once again produced fear and alarm and helped to shake the anti-unionist resolve of some members of the Ascendancy. What also helped was the unassailable position of William Pitt as Prime Minister. There was no chance now of an anti-unionist administration coming to power in Britain, and so Pitt controlled patronage.

The last point is particularly important. For in the end everything would turn on the vote in the Irish House of Commons, and Castlereagh was determined to ensure that it went the government's way. He prepared the ground by employing influence, pressure and bribery on a massive scale to ensure that MPs voted in favour of union. As a result some anti-unionist MPs were induced to change their minds or to give up their seats; and a flood of new MPs – around one-fifth of the total – entered the Irish House of Commons between January 1799 and January 1800.

Hence, when the Irish parliament met again in early 1800 to reconsider the government's motion in favour of union, it consented by a vote of 158 to 115. In the spring both houses of the Irish parliament accepted the detailed plans for the Act of Union, and, after a few minor amendments, so too did the Westminster parliament. The Act of Union received the royal assent in August 1800.

Why then did the Irish parliament agree in this way to its own extinction? For some observers at the time, this was entirely due to Castlereagh's flagrant use of corruption. As one opposition ballad put it:

1 How did they pass the Union?
   By perjury and fraud;
   By slaves who sold their land for gold
   As Judas sold his God ...
5 And thus was passed the Union
   By Pitt and Castlereagh;
   Could Satan send for such an end
   More worthy tools than they?

Yet most recent historians conclude that this is too simple a view. There was nothing exceptional about the methods employed by Castlereagh in 1799–1800, only about their scale. The anti-unionists won the first round against the government in 1799 because they were united in resistance to the principle of union; they then failed because they had no agreed alternative once it became apparent that the government was determined to push ahead with its plan. Their failure seems more important than corruption in the government victory.

e) Terms

By the Act of Union, the 'United Kingdom of Great Britain and Ireland' was established on 1 January 1801. The separate Irish parliament disappeared, and Ireland was incorporated into the British parliamentary system. To the House of Lords were added four Irish spiritual lords and 28 temporal lords elected for life by the whole body of Irish peers. Ireland elected 100 MPs to the House of Commons: two for each county, two each for the cities of Dublin and Cork, one each for 31 other cities and boroughs, and one for the University of Dublin.

In spiritual matters the Churches of Ireland and England were united as the Established Church of England and Ireland. Free trade was established between the two countries, and (with a few minor exceptions) there were to be equal commercial privileges. The financial systems of the two countries were to remain separate for the time being. Ireland was to contribute two-seventeenths to the expenditure of the United Kingdom and Great Britain was to contribute fifteen-seventeenths. The legal systems and laws of the two countries remained as they were.

f) Consequences

The high hopes of the supporters of the Union went largely unful-filled. There were a number of reasons for this. In the first place, the political incorporation of Ireland into the United Kingdom was a half-hearted affair. In many ways Ireland was still treated as a separate country – as 'a half-alien dependency', in one historian's phrase. The Viceroy remained as the Crown's representative; the Castle continued to administer Ireland; and the Chief Secretary dealt with Irish affairs in the House of Commons on behalf of the British government, most of whose members remained unconcerned with the realities of Irish life. The Protestant Ascendancy therefore continued to control Ireland and run its local politics as they had done before 1801. Yet the anti-unionists soon accepted the new dispensation.

All this meant that Irish Protestantism – especially the Ulster Presbyterians, who now built up strong economic and religious links with England – came to be identified with loyalty to the Union. By contrast, the Catholics soon became increasingly anti-unionist and began to develop a strong sense of their own separate Irish religious and national identity. They felt betrayed when Union was not fol-lowed by Catholic emancipation. Pitt's plan for emancipation immediately after union was foiled by the obduracy of King George III (who argued that it would betray his Coronation oath to defend the Church of England), and Pitt preferred to resign in 1801 rather than engage in a struggle with the Crown over the issue. Nor were the economic advantages for Ireland proclaimed by William Pitt realised. It soon became apparent, in the age of the British industrial revol-ution, that Irish industries (with the exception of Ulster linen) had no chance of competing effectively with those of Great Britain. Nor was Ireland regarded as a sound and safe field for investment by British bankers and businessmen. Far from economic resources flowing from England to Ireland (as Pitt had prophesied) the traffic proved to be all the other way, as rapid population growth led to large-scale emi-gration from Ireland to England and Scotland.

The religious and national divide in Ireland, contrary to the hopes of men like William Pitt, was therefore strengthened rather than weakened as a result of the Act of Union. An upsurge of agrarian out-rage and crime prompted Sir Arthur Wellesley (later the Duke of Wellington), the Chief Secretary in 1807, to insist that Ireland 'must be considered to be enemy's country'. It was in these circumstances that a new, outstanding leader of Catholic Ireland at last emerged in the 1820s in the person of Daniel O'Connell, prepared to use popu-lar power to challenge the will of the British state.

Summary Diagram

The Making of the Act of Union, 1800

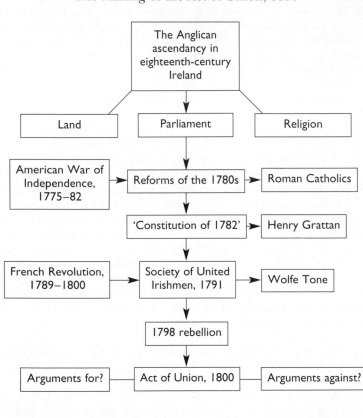

Working on Chapter 2

It is essential to make brief notes (divided into landownership, religion, and politics) on the period of the Anglican Ascendancy. More detailed notes on the Act of Union are then required. These should emphasise the arguments for and against; clearly explain the terms of the Act; and (which is more difficult) consider how successful the Act was up to the 1820s.

Answering structured and essay questions on Chapter 2

Questions on the Act of Union tend to be concerned, in one form or another, with its origins, aims and results. Consider the following example:

1 **a)** Describe the main features of the 'Ascendancy' in eighteenth-century Ireland.
  b) What were the main discontents that lay behind the rebellion of 1798?
  c) What deficiencies of the existing system in Ireland was the Act of Union of 1800 designed to overcome?

Notice the way in which the third part of this stepped question builds upon the factual contents of the first two.

A typical essay question on this area is as follows:

2 What were the aims of the supporters of the Act of Union of 1800, and how successfully were they realised in the first half of the nineteenth century?

A good answer to this question would provide an introduction outlining the special problems of the Anglo-Irish relationship in the second half of the eighteenth century. Two major sections should then follow on 'aims' and 'results'. You would have to decide what topics to include in the first section. 'Security' and 'politics', certainly. What about 'religion' or 'economic policy'? In the second section you are faced with the key word 'successfully' – which crops up in so many history questions. How do you estimate success? Success for whom? What sort of success – political, economic, religious? These are the sorts of question you must think carefully about.

Source-based questions on Chapter 2

1 The Act of Union: Arguments For
Read the quotations from the speeches of Lord Clare and William Pitt on pages 23 and 24, and answer the following questions.

a) Who were 'the old inhabitants of Ireland' mentioned by Lord Clare, and what were their main 'discontents' in the eighteenth century? (*5 marks*)
b) What practical protection does Pitt expect England to provide for Ireland after Union? (*3 marks*)
c) What specific economic benefits does Pitt expect Union to bring to Ireland? (*5 marks*)
d) What are the 'feuds and divisions which now distract the country' referred to by Pitt? Why does he expect Union to alter this? (*7 marks*)
e) Estimate the importance of the arguments deployed by Clare and Pitt in securing the passage of the Act of Union. (*10 marks*)

2 The Act of Union: Arguments Against
Read the extract from the speech of John Foster on page 24, and the ballad on page 26, and answer the following questions.

a) What is significant about the date '1782' mentioned by Foster? What was 'the present war'? (*5 marks*)

b) What examples can be given to show that Ireland had 'risen in civilisation, wealth and manufactures' since 1782? (*5 marks*)

c) Was Foster justified in referring to Ireland's 'free Constitution' before 1800? (*5 marks*)

d) What part was played in the passage of the Act of Union by Lord Castlereagh, mentioned in the ballad? What was meant by 'perjury and fraud'? (*7 marks*)

e) How strong were the arguments of the anti-unionists, and why were they unable to prevent Union? (*8 marks*)

3 Daniel O'Connell, 'the Liberator'

POINTS TO CONSIDER

This chapters covers important events in Anglo-Irish history, including the mobilisation of mass support in the Catholic Association and the passing of the Emancipation Act and other reforms. But it is important to focus not just on what happened but (i) on why and (ii) on the consequences of events. Pay particular attention to the role of Daniel O'Connell, asking wherein lay his importance, and on the alternative strategy of Robert Peel. You also need to grapple with the contentious issue of how we should evaluate O'Connell's historical stature.

KEY DATES

1823 May   formation of the Catholic Association
1828 July   O'Connell elected MP for County Clare
1829 April   Roman Catholic Emancipation Act
1833   Coercion Act
1835   (February) Litchfield House Compact: an alliance of Whigs and Irish lasting until 1840
1840   Repeal Association founded by O'Connell
1843   (October) Repeal meeting at Clontarf banned
1846   Young Ireland leaders left the Catholic Association
1847   Death of O'Connell

1 The Campaign for Catholic Emancipation

> **KEY ISSUES** What special circumstances enabled O'Connell to bring about Emancipation in 1829? How significant was this achievement?

a) The Rise of O'Connell

The early years of the nineteenth century were a depressing time for the supporters of Catholic Emancipation. In England there was still much popular prejudice against Roman Catholics, for political as well as religious reasons. Though the old idea that Catholics were actively plotting to overthrow the Hanoverian dynasty had faded, most members of the political classes believed that it would be unwise to give full political rights to Roman Catholics. Were not their loyalties divided, between allegiance to the Crown and support for the Pope at Rome? The Prince Regent, like his father, King George III, before him, maintained an obstinate opposition to Catholic emancipation during the years of his Regency, 1811–20. Thus, before the 1820s, all the bills introduced into the House of Commons by supporters of Emancipation were rejected by large majorities.

In Ireland too the Catholic cause made little headway. The leaders of the Emancipation campaign, who were mainly members of the Roman Catholic upper class, were unwilling to seek active popular support and were cautious and conciliatory in their dealings with the authorities. They were even willing to support a compromise Emancipation Bill which, while granting political and civil rights to Catholics, included what became known as the 'veto'. This would

PROFILE: DANIEL O'CONNELL (1775–1847)

-Profile-

Daniel O'Connell was born on 6 August 1775 in Kerry in the west of Ireland, as a member of the Roman Catholic gentry class. His roots were therefore deep in the Catholic and Celtic traditions of rural Ireland. Irish was his first language, though he soon abandoned it for English, the language of the dominant nation. He was educated in France for a number of years, and then studied law at Lincoln's Inn in London between 1794 and 1796 in order to qualify as a barrister. In London he was strongly influenced by the ideas of the English radicals, especially William Godwin, the author of *Political Justice*, imbibing a belief in political and religious liberty and, above all, in the importance of moral, rather than physical, force in affecting change. These were principles which remained with him throughout his life, though he later successfully used the *threat* of violence. Unlike many English radicals, however, he retained his Roman Catholic religion.

After London he studied at Dublin and was eventually called to the Irish Bar in 1798. He built up a large and profitable practice as a barrister travelling around the Irish legal circuit and coming into touch with the people and problems of Catholic Ireland, where he became known as 'The Counsellor'. All this helped to prepare him for his future political career.

Daniel O'Connell first came into prominence in Irish politics as one of the framers of the Petition of 1805 in favour of the removal of Roman Catholic disabilities, an appeal rejected by the

British government. Then he became the leader of the radical wing on the new Catholic Board which he set up in 1811. He founded the Catholic Association in 1823 and was the major figure behind Catholic Emancipation in 1829. Gladstone was to call him 'the greatest popular leader whom the world has ever seen'.

allow the British government the right to vet ecclesiastical appointments to the Roman Catholic Church in the United Kingdom in order to ensure that only 'loyal' clerics were appointed. This timorous attitude was vigorously denounced by Daniel O'Connell. He rejected the veto, believing that it was vital to maintain the freedom of the Catholic Church from interference by a British government. To do otherwise would be a retrograde step, back to the days of the penal code.

In 1821 a Catholic Emancipation Bill (including the veto) actually obtained a majority in the House of Commons, but was rejected by the Lords. In many ways this was a turning point for O'Connell and the cause he represented. 'Twenty years ... have passed away', he said, 'and we are still slaves'. Faced with the permanent hostility of the Crown and the House of Lords, he believed that the Emancipation movement in Ireland must now reconsider its aims and methods if the deadlock was to be broken. That was now to be accomplished with the formation of the Catholic Association in 1823–4.

b) The Catholic Association

The Catholic Association was formed by O'Connell and his supporters in 1823 as a constitutional organisation for the achievement of Catholic civil and political rights. However, it only expanded when in 1824, in a master stroke of policy, O'Connell introduced the famous 'Catholic Rent' of one penny a month for supporters, instead of the high subscription originally proposed. This enabled the Association to become a truly national organisation with strong roots among the peasantry, and turned the old ineffective pressure group into what has been called 'the crusade of an irresistible mass movement'.

The main aim of the Catholic Association, like the old Catholic Board, was Emancipation. But it also attempted to embrace a wider range of issues, such as electoral reform, reform of the Church of Ireland, tenants' rights and economic development, in order to advance the interests of the whole Catholic community. Though membership of the Association was not confined to Catholics, O'Connell did aim at making the Irish Catholic Church an integral part of the whole movement, since, as he rightly realised, the role of the parish priests was of crucial importance in spreading the message and helping to collect the Catholic rent.

Indeed, the Catholic rent was to become the mainstay of the work of the Association as a whole. Its collection was enormously successful: £20,000 was raised in the first nine months alone in 1824–5, and £35,000 was collected between 1826 and 1829. Some of this vast sum – primarily as a gesture towards the Church – was used for educational and other communal purposes; but the bulk of the money was used to finance the Association's work as a national organisation of protest and agitation. The Association was run from Dublin by a committee of O'Connell and his friends and supporters, who directed and encouraged activities at regional and local levels. An important and effective part of the Association's work was the organisation of great open-air public meetings which were often addressed by O'Connell himself. He proved to be an outstanding public speaker: his background and his work as a lawyer meant that he knew his audiences, and his magnificent voice and clear, conversational style of oratory enabled him to build up a marvellous rapport with the Catholic masses. For the peasantry in particular, O'Connell seemed the incarnation of their hopes and ambitions, not only in a material but in an almost religious sense. He became known as 'the Deliverer'. In turn, the peasant traditions of secret societies and local agitation helped to reinforce the work of the Association at grassroots level.

As a public orator O'Connell spoke with two voices. On the one hand, in speaking to his fellow countrymen, he demanded justice for Ireland, which meant Emancipation and the redress of Catholic grievances, to be obtained by peaceful means. But at the same time he was addressing the British government. Here, in a series of veiled threats, he hinted that British failure to yield to the Association's demands could lead to mass disobedience, possible violence and eventual separation. This policy of 'brinkmanship' was dangerous but, as later events were to show, also successful.

Apart from its innovative ways of raising money, its organisational work and its great public meetings, the Catholic Association also used the press and public posters to build up support. In many ways, therefore, the Association was a sophisticated political organisation: 'a pioneer ... of mass constitutional politics and pacific popular democracy', in the words of Oliver MacDonagh, O'Connell's major biographer. Geographically, its main area of support proved to be in Munster in south-west Ireland, and later in the south-east; the north, where O'Connell was seen by the powerful Protestant community as a Roman Catholic demagogue, proved to be largely barren territory. Three main Catholic groups provided organisational support for the Association: the urban middle classes – particularly lawyers – who hoped to gain most, economically and professionally, from Emancipation; the rural middle classes, whose links with the peasantry and local politics were particularly important; and the parish priests, who became the most important emissaries of the Association at local level.

The rapid progress of the Association and O'Connell's often belli-cose language at public meetings alarmed the authorities, and he was arrested in 1824 on a charge of incitement to rebellion, though the prosecution failed. In 1825 the government did suppress the Association, but it was soon re-organised by O'Connell. In 1825 too another Emancipation Bill passed through the House of Commons, but was again rejected by the House of Lords. The deadlock therefore still remained.

The following year, however, saw the beginning of a new phase in the history of the Emancipation campaign. 1826 was an election year, and the Association decided to intervene directly and deliberately in the Irish elections. This time, in unprecedented fashion, it called upon the voters in selected counties to support only pro-Emancipation candidates, whether they were Whigs or Tories. This meant that the Catholic 40-shilling freeholders (those who possessed a 'freehold' worth at least 40 shillings a year in rental value, which entitled them to vote) – the mainstay of the county electorate and normally a deferential group – were being urged to defy their Protestant landlords. A number were indeed prepared to do so. The meticulous organisation of the Catholic voters by the Association with the co-operation of the local priests achieved a considerable success: four pro-Emancipation candidates were returned. The most remark-able contest was at Waterford where the English landowners, the Beresfords, had controlled the seat for generations. On this occasion Lord George Beresford was defeated by Villiers Stuart, an ally of O'Connell's.

It was the fact that the Catholic voters in these counties had the backing of a powerful national organisation in the form of the Catholic Association that enabled them to defy their landlords with relative impunity. The Association, proclaimed R.L. Shiel, one of O'Connell's lieutenants, was now 'master of the representation of Ireland'. The lessons of the 1826 general election were not lost on the British government either. As Robert Peel (Home Secretary) wrote: 'the instrument of deference and supremacy had been converted into a weapon fatal to the authority of the landlord'. O'Connell himself was now the key figure in Irish politics. It was at thus point that the Tory Prime Minister, Lord Liverpool, resigned, precipitating a crisis that profoundly affected the situation in Ireland.

c) The Emancipation Crisis 1828–9

Liverpool's retirement in 1827 brought to a head the divisions within the Cabinet over Catholic Emancipation. On one side were its oppo-nents, notably Robert Peel and the Duke of Wellington, who, as sup-porters of the rights and privileges of the Established Church of England, were opposed to Emancipation on grounds of principle. On the other were those members of the Cabinet, led by George

Canning, who supported Emancipation for pragmatic reasons: it would help to bind Ireland to the Union, and enable the government to deal more effectively with the problems of that country.

On Liverpool's retirement Canning became Prime Minister, but his outlook on the Catholic question led Peel and Wellington to refuse to join his ministry. It was not until Wellington himself became Prime Minister in January 1828 (following the premature death of Canning and a brief interlude under Lord Goderich) that Peel agreed to resume office as Home Secretary and second-in-command in the government. Unfortunately, the elevation of the reactionary Duke to the premiership soon led to the resignation of Canning's former supporters from the new government. The Tory party was now in almost complete disarray, and in no fit state therefore to deal with a major crisis. But the repeal of the Test and Corporations Acts in February 1828 (which ended all legal restrictions on the civil rights of Dissenters) at the instigation of the Whig leader, Lord John Russell, was bound to make it difficult for the Tory leaders to ignore the issue of Catholic Emancipation. It was, however, a by-election in an obscure parliamentary constituency in Ireland that now brought matters to a head.

i) The County Clare Election 1828

Early in 1828 Vesey Fitzgerald was appointed President of the Board of Trade, and, as was customary at that time, had to stand for re-election – in his case in his constituency of County Clare in the west of Ireland. Fitzgerald was in fact a popular landlord and a supporter of emancipation; but, in an act of supreme audacity, O'Connell decided to stand as a candidate for the seat himself.

O'Connell's candidature at County Clare presented the government with an intolerable dilemma. Since O'Connell was a Roman Catholic he would be unable to take his seat in the House of Commons if elected without a change in the law – in effect, Catholic Emancipation. Yet to oppose his right to enter the Commons would run the risk of widespread public disorder and violence in Ireland, with the unenviable prospect of further Catholic candidacies at elections in the future. In the event things worked out exactly as O'Connell had anticipated. With the backing of the Catholic Association and the local priests, the Catholic voters were prepared once again to defy their landlords, and O'Connell won an easy victory in July (with 2,057 votes to Fitzgerald's 982). The latter wrote to Peel that O'Connell's organisation was 'so complete and so formidable that no man can contemplate without alarm what is to follow in this wretched country'.

'This business', wrote one English MP of the Clare election, 'must bring the Catholic question to a crisis and conclusion'. So it turned out. The Duke of Wellington, as a soldier and ex-Irish Secretary, took the threat of violence seriously, and concluded that on purely practical grounds emancipation must be conceded, even if this meant bullying the king, browbeating the House of Lords and facing the prospect of a Tory revolt in the House of Commons. Peel, after some hesitation, accepted the logic of the duke's case, and agreed to shoulder the burden of getting the proposed bill through the House of Commons.

ii) The Roman Catholic Emancipation Act 1829

The Emancipation Bill passed through the House of Commons early in 1829 as a result of the support of the Whigs and liberal Tories (142 Tory MPs voted against); and the demoralised Lords, not daring to defy the duke, subsequently passed it by a two-to-one majority. King George IV (formerly the Prince Regent) sulkily acquiesced, and the bill became law in April 1829. The influence of the Protestant supporters of emancipation in the House of Commons was essential to the passing of the Act, and they were helped by the disunity of the Tory party. But the lion's share of the victory was, rightly, claimed by O'Connell, who now earned the title of 'the Liberator'.

The Roman Catholic Emancipation Act of 1829 was a simple one, largely due to Peel's insistence. It granted virtually full civil and political rights to Roman Catholics, which meant that they could now become MPs and occupy the highest positions in the state (with a few minor exceptions, such as the office of Lord Chancellor). On the other hand, in a gesture of political spite, the franchise qualification in Ireland was raised from a 40-shilling freehold to a £10 household suffrage, and this cut the Irish electorate to one-sixth of its former size.

O'Connell welcomed the bill with enthusiasm. 'Peel's bill for Emancipation', he wrote to his wife in March 1829, 'is good – very good; frank, direct, complete; no veto, no control'. He was not overworried by the electoral restrictions, since, though he had mobilised them, he believed that the 40-shilling freeholders were still too much under the control of the landlords. What was much more important were the opportunities opened up by the Emancipation Act for Catholic advancement in politics, the professions and government service – and he believed that this was bound to lead to the eventual destruction of the Protestant Ascendancy in Ireland. In that sense the Act was, as the Liberator proclaimed to a friend, 'one of the greatest triumphs recorded in history – a bloodless revolution'. Most modern historians agree. '1829', writes J.C. Beckett, 'proved a more important turning point in the history of modern Ireland than 1800'. Nevertheless, fundamental change in Ireland after 1829 was slow; and indeed since the Emancipation Act was regarded by Irish Protestants as primarily a Catholic victory, sectarianism increased. This meant that in practice, despite O'Connell's protestations to the contrary, the achievement of the 1829 Act marks another stage in the identification of Irish nationalism with Catholicism. 'Our politics', as an Irish land agent wrote only a few years later, 'have little or nothing to do with any general principle or feeling save that of Catholic versus Protestant'.

In Great Britain, however, the Emancipation Act was followed by swift and dramatic changes in politics. It helped to precipitate the break-up of the old Tory Party and the rise of a new Conservative Party; the triumph of the Whigs and their allies at the general election of 1830; and, subsequently, the passage of the Great Reform Act of 1832. These years also saw the emergence of an Irish party in the House of Commons, led by O'Connell, who was able to use his commanding position as leader of a small but significant third party to play off Whigs against Conservatives and thus extract reforms for Ireland. But O'Connell proved to be more than just a parliamentary politician. The County Clare election had shown what could be achieved by the power of mass opinion in Ireland, organised by political activists and under clerical influence. 'The policy of brinkmanship', as one historian puts it, 'received the seal of success'. What had been achieved once, as both O'Connell and his enemies perceived, could perhaps be achieved again. This meant that 'the Irish question', as the years after 1829 were to prove up to the hilt, could never be reduced to a purely parliamentary dimension.

2 O'Connell and the Whigs, 1830–40

> **KEY ISSUE** How fruitful was the alliance forged between O'Connell and the Whig government in the 1830s?

After the success of the Emancipation campaign O'Connell was able to give up the law and devote his whole time to politics, as he received a gift of £20,000 from Irish Catholics in recognition of his great services, and further regular payments thereafter, known as 'the O'Connell Tribute'. He now possessed a dual position as both an Irish national leader and a British parliamentary politician: his immediate task was to decide what role to adopt. Should he concentrate on a policy of repeal of the Act of Union and rely on another campaign in Ireland to ensure its success? Or should he use his new position in the House of Commons to press for immediate reforms for Ireland? O'Connell's long-term aim was clearly Repeal. 'I have an ultimate object,' he had proclaimed in 1813, 'it is the Repeal of the Union and the restoration to Old Ireland of her independence'. But the Liberator was primarily an opportunist in politics. He was never prepared to come down firmly on the side of either Repeal or Reform; and in practice he veered from one to the other as and when circumstances dictated, and often spoke with the voice of Repeal in Ireland and of Reform in England.

However, it soon became clear in the years immediately following emancipation that it would be difficult to mount a new mass campaign in Ireland in favour of Repeal, although some sporadic agitation was organised. In the first place, many members of the Catholic middle classes wanted to see some of the fruits of emancipation in terms of jobs and opportunities as soon as possible, and this implied reform. A number of leading Catholic bishops also supported a policy of 'reform first'. Furthermore, the actions of the Catholic peasantry – many of whom had lost the vote and most of whom felt frustrated by the lack of any real change in their conditions – demanded immediate action. Their refusal to pay their tithes to the Anglican Church led to the outbreak of a vicious 'tithe war' in the 1830s. It was accompanied by the acceleration of rural crime and outrage, the forcible and generally unsuccessful attempts by the authorities to collect the tithe with the use of police and soldiers, and the virtual breakdown of law and order in many parts of Ireland. In 1832, for example, there were 242 murders, 300 attempted murders, and 560 cases of arson throughout Ireland. For the new Whig government after 1830 the immediate priority in Ireland was the restoration of law and order, a policy which, implicitly, many leaders of the Roman Catholic laity and clergy were prepared to accept.

Thus, from O'Connell's point of view, the situation in parliament seemed more propitious, even though he was treated with open contempt as an outsider by many MPs. In the general election of 1830, 30 Irish (O'Connellite) MPs were returned to the House of Commons, and emerged as an influential third party. Their support for Earl Grey, the Whig leader, was important in getting the Great Reform Bill through the House of Commons in 1831–2. But the terms of the Act itself were disappointing to the Irish. The vote was not restored to the 40-shilling freeholders, and Ireland only obtained five new MPs. Nevertheless, in the post-reform general election in 1833, the O'Connellites emerged with 39 MPs, and thus became the largest bloc of Irish MPs in the House of Commons. However, the Liberator was not yet prepared to co-operate fully with the Whigs, an attitude which seemed even more justified when they passed a new Coercion Act for Ireland in 1833, to last for just one year. This was one of the toughest pieces of law-and-order legislation to affect Ireland in the nineteenth century. It gave the authorities wide powers of arbitrary arrest and imprisonment and control of public meetings. The Act did succeed in diminishing the amount of violent crime and stifling Repeal agitation, and even received the tacit support of Irish Catholic bishops. O'Connell, however, denounced its authors as 'the base, brutal and bloody Whigs'.

Yet, despite the rhetoric, there were good reasons for the two parties to come together, for the Whigs had already begun a programme of Irish reform. In 1832 Stanley, as Irish Secretary, introduced a system of 'national schools' which, although it failed to satisfy his aim of overcoming religious sectarianism, did much to attack basic illiteracy. In the following year the Irish Church Act was passed. This reformed the unrepresentative Church of Ireland by abolishing ten sees, including two archbishoprics; and it was suggested that the sequestered church funds obtained from this be used for secular purposes. Whatever the defects of this legislation, it soon became apparent to O'Connell that the new reformed parliament was no more in favour of Repeal than the old one had been. A resolution in favour of Repeal in 1834 was defeated in the Commons by a massive vote of 523 to 38 – with only one British MP voting in favour. Even English liberals and radicals, it appeared, were averse to the prospect of a separate, Roman Catholic-dominated Irish parliament. For O'Connell, therefore, if Repeal was ruled out, co-operation with the Whigs offered the prospect of a continuation of Irish reform.

The Whigs were even more enthusiastic for Irish support, for by 1834 they needed all the help they could get if they were to continue in office. In November of that year, owing to disputes arising principally out of the sequestration clauses of the Irish Church Act, which offended many Anglicans, two Cabinet ministers resigned and were supported by some 40 backbenchers. As a result, Earl Grey gave up his post as Prime Minister and was succeeded by Lord Melbourne. The whole incident shows the new centrality of Irish issues in British politics. Melbourne too found it difficult to carry on, and, in collusion with King William IV, arranged for his own dismissal. Sir Robert Peel, the Conservative leader, was then appointed Prime Minister, as head of a minority administration. In the general election which shortly followed in January 1835 the Conservatives gained more than 100 seats, and Peel pushed ahead with his own plans. But he was playing for time, for his party still remained a minority in the House of Commons despite their remarkable recovery. If the opposition groups could combine their forces, the Conservative government's fate was sealed. That is exactly what did happen at the famous Litchfield House Compact, made between the Whigs, Radicals, and Irish in February 1835: 'one of the most decisive events in British political history between 1832 and 1847', as it has been called. Within a few weeks the government was defeated in the House of Commons, Peel resigned, and Melbourne came back as Prime Minister. Thus began a Whig-Irish alliance that lasted until 1840.

Fears of more unrest in Ireland, together with an acceptance of the legitimacy of many Irish grievances, made the Whigs amenable to the case for further Irish reform. A new spirit of fairness and impartiality was now applied to the administration of Ireland, mainly due to the efforts of Thomas Drummond, the Irish Under-Secretary. Catholics were appointed to high offices in the Irish judiciary and the Castle; a new national police force was established, with Catholics encouraged to join; and the political powers of the extremist Protestant Orange Order were curbed. Drummond insisted that the police and military were no longer to be used automatically to defend the claims of the landlords or to collect tithes – 'property has its duties as well as its rights', as he said in a famous phrase. In fact, as far as the tithe question was concerned, an Act of 1838 introduced a compromise solution by which the tithe now became a fixed additional rent charge, payable by the landlord.

Lord John Russell, as Home Secretary, also tried to introduce into Ireland a number of major English reforms. A new workhouse system based on the principles of the 1834 Poor Law Act was set up, and the 1840 Corporations Act attempted to apply to Ireland the major features of the 1835 Act which had reformed English urban government. Admittedly the system of poor relief subsequently proved to be inadequate and, due to the opposition of the House of Lords, the Irish Corporations Act was much narrower than its English counterpart, being based on a £10 household suffrage, rather than (as in England) the much wider ratepayer suffrage, and with more limited powers, so that control of the police, for example, was excluded. In addition, the 1840 Act abolished 58 Irish corporations. Nevertheless, the new regime in Irish local government did offer opportunities to Catholics. The O'Connellites won control of 10 local councils, and in 1841 O'Connell was elected Lord Mayor of Dublin, the first Catholic to hold that position since the reign of James II. Catholics were also appointed as sheriffs, magistrates, and members of Poor Law Boards of Guardians.

The year 1840 marks in effect the end of the Whig-Irish alliance. Despite O'Connell's initial enthusiasm, the Irish Catholics seemed to gain little of real substance from a decade of Whig reform. Ireland was still treated differently from England, and the power of the Protestant Ascendancy there still remained unbroken; it was the Whigs who appeared to gain most from the alliance. The contemporary description of the O'Connellites as 'the Irish tail' to the Whig parliamentary party was not inappropriate. For while the Whigs obtained the one thing they vitally needed – Irish parliamentary support – O'Connell was forced to compromise time and time again in order to keep the government in power. Moreover, his concentration on parliamentary politics after 1835 to some extent cut him off from his Irish roots. This was reflected in the decline of the 'O'Connell Tribute' and the waning of his own personal influence in Ireland.

The Liberator had always insisted that 'if that experiment failed, I would come back with tenfold force to the Repeal'. The signal for the new policy came in 1840 with the formation of the National Repeal Association and his break with the Whigs. A mass agitation in favour of Repeal became virtually certain when, as a result of the Conservatives' triumph at the general election of 1841, Sir Robert Peel became Prime Minister. For, apart from other considerations, there was a personal antipathy between O'Connell and Peel which went back to the latter's Irish Secretaryship nearly 30 years before, when the two men had almost fought a duel. For Peel, O'Connell was still 'the great blackguard', while for the free-and-easy Irish leader the Prime Minister was a cold and callous Englishman whose 'smile was like the silver plate on a coffin'.

3 The Repeal Campaign, 1840–4

> **KEY ISSUE** Why did O'Connell's attempts to secure Repeal fail, whereas earlier his Emancipation campaign had succeeded?

O'Connell's main efforts after 1840 were concentrated on a national Repeal campaign in Ireland. 'Repeal', he proclaimed, 'is the sole basis which the people will accept … Repeal alone is and must be the grand basis of all future operations, hit or miss, win or lose'. In many ways it resembled, although on a much larger scale, the campaign in favour of Catholic Emancipation in the 1820s. Repeal rested upon the support of two major groups: the peasantry, to whom it seemed to offer the diminution of the landlords' power, and the Catholic Church. As far as the Church was concerned, O'Connell could rely once again on the loyalty of the parish priests; but this time many bishops were prepared to come out openly in support, notably Archbishop MacHale, the most powerful man in the Irish Catholic Church. This did mean, however, that the Liberator was forced to go along with the Church's views on contentious questions such as education, which was bound to antagonise Protestants. One difference, however, between the present campaign and the earlier one, was that this time the Catholic middle classes were less committed, since (as we have seen) many of them were more concerned with the immediate material gains to be obtained from the Union, rather than the problematic future advantages of Repeal. On the other hand, O'Connell did have the support of a small but significant group of more extreme nationalists, known as 'Young Ireland', led by the Protestant, Thomas Davis.

What, however, did Repeal mean? On this fundamental point O'Connell was vague and ambiguous. If it meant a return to the status quo before 1800, then this implied the re-establishment of the Irish parliament, though on a more representative basis. This would then be followed by the enactment of measures to improve conditions for the Irish people, though to allay the fears of the propertied classes O'Connell went out of his way to stress that this would not mean any 'social revolution'. But what exactly would be done about social, economic and religious affairs? And what powers would be enjoyed by the new parliament in a new Anglo-Irish relationship? A speech by the Liberator to a mass audience on 14 May 1843, was typical.

1 My first object is to get Ireland for the Irish ... Old Ireland and liberty!
That is what I am struggling for ... What numberless advantages would
not the Irish enjoy if they possessed their own country? A domestic
parliament would encourage Irish manufactures ... Irish commerce and
5 protect Irish agriculture. The labourer, the artizan, and the shopkeeper
would all be benefitted by the repeal of the union ... They say we want
separation from England, but what I want is to prevent separation taking
place ... what motive could we have to separate if we obtain all these
blessings? ... I want you to do nothing that is not open and legal, but if
10 the people unite with me and follow my advice it is impossible not to
get the Repeal ... there was no pursuit of Roman Catholic interests as
opposed to Protestant ... the object in view was the benefit of the
whole nation.

The vagueness and inconsistencies in such speeches have led some
historians to refuse to take seriously O'Connell's support for Repeal
as a genuine political aim. They have suggested that the whole Repeal
campaign was merely an attempt to blackmail the British government
into granting further and more fundamental reforms within the
framework of the Union. 'He used Repeal', writes Oliver MacDonagh,
'as a popular rallying-cry, a mode of intimidating governments and a
hoped-for bargaining counter'.

The Repeal campaign was financed by the 'Repeal Rent', which was
similar to the 'Catholic Rent' of the earlier campaign, and brought in
ample funds; and this enabled an efficient, national movement to be

King O'Connell at Tara – *Punch*, 1844

established again. The outstanding characteristic of the new campaign in the early 1840s was the organisation of 'monster meetings', strictly controlled by O'Connell on a peaceful basis: 'the atmosphere' (writes one historian) 'was a mixture of fair, football game and evangelical revival'. These tactics did lead to a massive mobilisation of the Irish Catholics, especially in the key year 1843; and overall around three to four million people may have attended these meetings, representing the pinnacle of the Liberator's career as a popular leader. Their aim was, he said, 'to convince our enemies ... I want to make England feel her weakness if she refuses to give the justice we require'. Though occasionally O'Connell hinted at the use of force, fundamentally the Repeal Association was a vast pressure group which aimed (like the contemporary Anti-Corn Law League, with which it was often compared) to arouse and canalise opinion through propaganda and large-scale public agitation, and thus force the government to repeal the Act of Union. This was, after all, a tactic which had worked successfully against another Tory government in 1828–9.

But Peel was in a much stronger position than Wellington had been during the Emancipation crisis. As Prime Minister in 1841 he commanded a strong, united and confident Conservative party, with a large majority in the House of Commons. Hence he was not dependent on the Irish members (as the Whigs had been after 1835) to maintain himself in power. Besides, O'Connellites were down to 19 MPs after the general election of 1841, mainly due to the decline of O'Connell's personal influence in Ireland as a result of tying himself to the Whigs. Moreover, the Irish electorate was no longer so formidable, owing to the earlier disenfranchisement of the 40-shilling freeholders. Nor was O'Connell's support as united as it appeared. Middle-class Catholics, as we have seen, had their own doubts about Repeal and were worried by the radical implications of a mass agitation. 'Young Ireland' too (as later events showed) differed sharply with the Liberator over tactics and long-term aims. By contrast, all shades of Protestant opinion in England and Ireland were totally united in their opposition to Repeal.

To begin with Peel was prepared to tolerate the Repeal movement so long as it remained strictly within the law; and he therefore played down the alarmist clamour of the Lord-Lieutenant and the Irish Protestants for immediate suppression of the Association. But, in a set speech to the Commons in May 1843, the Prime Minister spelled out the implications of his support for the Union. 'Deprecating as I do all war, but, above all, civil war, yet there is no alternative which I do not think preferable to the dismemberment of this empire.' At the same time the army was strengthened in Ireland. Clearly, on this occasion the government was determined not to back down.

As far as the Repeal campaign was concerned, things came to a head in the autumn of 1843. The momentum of the movement itself pushed O'Connell and other leaders into more threatening postures, with hints of mass unrest and military action. Peel waited for the right tactical moment to arrive, and then acted suddenly and swiftly. The monster meeting planned by O'Connell to take place at Clontarf on 7 October was banned by the authorities. The Irish leader accepted the decision peacefully, and his followers acquiesced, though many of them were disappointed and resentful.

'Clontarf' marks the effective end of the Repeal campaign. Yet the Liberator believed that not all was lost. The work of the Repeal Association, he suggested, had at least 'aroused the English nation from slumber. Our grievances are beginning to be admitted by all parties ... to be afflicting'. It was followed by a new period of Irish reform, initiated this time by the Irish leader's formidable adversary, Sir Robert Peel.

4 Peel and Irish Reform

KEY ISSUE How viable was Peel's strategy of reform in Ireland?

The lesson that Peel drew from the confrontation with O'Connell was that 'mere force ... will do nothing as a permanent remedy for the social ills of Ireland'. What he aimed at now was to build up in Catholic Ireland, especially among the middle classes, a feeling of confidence in the effectiveness and impartiality of government and the law, and thus reconcile the community to the benefits of the Union. Peel therefore continued the Whigs' policy of appointing suitable Catholics to official posts in Ireland, particularly in the judiciary. In 1844 he went further, and submitted to the Cabinet a programme of wide-ranging Irish reform covering such controversial topics as the franchise, landlord-tenant relations and, above all, Catholic education. One of Peel's main aims here was the need to break the 'powerful combination' (as he termed it) of O'Connell and the Catholic clergy – the dynamic behind Repeal. It was this, suggests a recent historian, that provided 'the cornerstone of his Irish policy'. It helps to explain the extraordinary, and unsuccessful, attempt by the British government to obtain the Pope's unequivocal condemnation of the political activities of the Irish priesthood.

But (apart from an act dealing with Catholic charities) the early part of Peel's programme was not very successful. A proposed new Franchise Bill, based on a £5 freeholder franchise, gained little support in the House of Commons and was dropped. A Bill for providing compensation to evicted Irish tenants, for improvements made to their holdings, was rejected by the House of Lords. These failures meant that Peel's reform programme came to depend more and more on the improvement of Irish education, and, in particular, on the vexed question of state support for Maynooth College.

Maynooth College had been established by the Irish parliament in 1795 as a training college for Catholic priests, and after the Act of Union it was supported financially by a small annual parliamentary grant. By the 1840s the college was clearly facing financial difficulties. In 1845, therefore, Peel decided to support a bill increasing the state grant to the college. His attitude, which represented a dramatic change in his views, was purely political: a greater injection of state funds and an improvement in the college's status would surely encourage the rise of a more 'respectable', less politicised, class of parish clergy. The penury and backwardness of the college, he argued, 'all combine to send forth a priesthood embittered rather than conciliated ... and connected ... with the lower classes of society'. Peel's Maynooth Bill, however, led to a storm of protest throughout the United Kingdom, since it seemed to provide state encouragement for the Roman Catholic Church. It also split the parliamentary Conservative party. In the end it only became law as a result of the firm support of the Irish in the House of Commons, and the Whigs in both houses of parliament.

With the Maynooth problem out of the way, Peel was able to pass on to the final phase of his Irish programme – the Colleges Bill. This passed fairly easily through parliament (though O'Connell opposed it) and led to the establishment of non-denominational university colleges at Belfast, Cork and Galway, thus providing wider and cheaper opportunities for higher education in Ireland, outside the Anglican foundation of Trinity College, Dublin. But the aim of interdenominational teaching was once again, as over the national schools in the 1830s, bedevilled by religious sectarianism, since the Catholic Church was not prepared to support colleges over whose teaching it had no control.

How important, then, was Peel's work for Ireland? His Irish reforms certainly displayed courage and resolution: as a recent historian of the subject writes, 'considered in the context of the time and the prejudices of his party they were remarkable'. But as a long-term solution to the problems of Ireland they were hopelessly inadequate. Nothing was done to alter the status of the Church of Ireland. Nothing was done for economic improvement or land reform. Mistrust of the British government and opposition to the Union still remained strong therefore among Irish Catholics. Inevitably, these feelings were exacerbated by the horrors and bitterness of the Great Famine of 1846–49 (discussed in the next chapter).

5 O'Connell: the Last Years

> **KEY ISSUES** Was O'Connell out of touch in his last years? How is
> his career best interpreted?

The successful banning of the Clontarf meeting was a turning point
in O'Connell's work for Ireland. Already ageing – he was now nearly
70 – the Liberator's career went into permanent decline after the
autumn of 1843. In May 1844 he was arrested and imprisoned for
incitement to violence, even though the verdict against him was soon
quashed by the House of Lords. Physically and mentally these events
took their toll. 'O'Connell', wrote Thomas Davis, the leader of 'Young
Ireland', 'will run no more risks ... from the day of his release the
cause will be going back and going down'.

The cause of Repeal was indeed worsened by O'Connell's personal
and ideological disputes with the leaders of 'Young Ireland'. They
resented the Liberator's opportunism – his commitment to parliamentary politics and alliances and support for reforms – as well as his
authoritarianism. As doctrinaire nationalists, Thomas Davis and his
colleagues were concerned above all with the raising of Irish national
consciousness, as the basis for an eventual independent Irish
Republic. They also differed with O'Connell over religion. Davis, a
Protestant, wanted religion kept out of the Repeal movement, but,
out of loyalty to his church and as a reward for their support in the
Repeal campaign, O'Connell felt duty bound to support the Catholic
bishops in their opposition to the new university colleges proposed by
Peel. The final break between the two groups of repealers came over
O'Connell's rigid commitment to peaceful agitation. In 1846 the
leaders of 'Young Ireland' came out in favour of the possible use of
force in support of Repeal (see page 62), and over this issue they were
either expelled from or left the Association.

By that time, however, Ireland was in the throes of the Great
Famine, and movements such as the Repeal Association – now divided
and weakened anyway – appeared increasingly remote and irrelevant.
O'Connell's attempt to revive the alliance with the Whigs after the fall
of Peel in June 1846 seemed one last futile gesture, especially as it was
the Whig government of Lord John Russell that was blamed for the
incompetence of the relief measures in Ireland during the grim
winter of 1846–7. The Liberator spoke for the last time in the House
of Commons in February 1847, and delivered a moving appeal for
parliament 'to act not only liberally but generously to find out the
means of putting a stop to this terrible disaster'. Then, aware of his
failing powers, he set off for Italy determined to spend his last days in
Rome. But he died at Genoa on 15 May 1847.

'No other single person', writes J.C. Beckett, 'has left such an
unmistakable mark on the history of Ireland'. What then were

O'Connell's achievements? His greatest success was undoubtedly the passing of the Roman Catholic Emancipation Act of 1829, which stemmed directly from his provocative candidature at the County Clare election in the summer of 1828. The Act not only remedied an old grievance and injustice but, by granting Roman Catholics virtually full civil and political rights, led gradually but inevitably to the destruction of the power of the Protestant Ascendancy in Ireland. More immediately, by granting Roman Catholics the right to become MPs, it led directly to the emergence of an Irish (O'Connellite) party in the House of Commons. As a result O'Connell became recognised – even by his opponents – as an outstanding parliamentarian and party leader.

The indirect results of these events were in some ways even more important. O'Connell and his party helped to bring the Irish question to the attention of the British parliament and the British people, and Irish claims and grievances now became an inextricable part of British domestic politics. Moreover, as one historian of the Irish party writes: 'Whatever the final judgement on O'Connell's party, there can be no doubt of its success as a political pressure group'. This success was seen in the Irish reforms passed by the sympathetic Whig governments of Grey and Melbourne, though (as we have seen) their need for Irish parliamentary support was also an important factor in explaining their support for reform. Despite his personal hostility to O'Connell, and the fact that he commanded an independent Conservative majority in the House of Commons, Sir Robert Peel too was prepared to support a measure of Irish reform. Indeed, it was over an issue directly affected by events in Ireland – the repeal of the Corn Laws in 1846 – that Peel sacrificed his political career and broke the unity of his party.

Recent historians have also emphasised the importance of the methods pursued by O'Connell, via the Catholic Association and, later, the Repeal Association. Both movements appealed consciously to all classes in Ireland; and both aimed deliberately at the peaceful organisation of mass opinion to change the law. 'O'Connell', it has been said, 'chose to use extra-parliamentary means to achieve constitutional ends'. By their use of such devices as popular fund-raising, large-scale public meetings, national organisation and leadership, and the involvement of local activists, the two Associations were the forerunners of modern political pressure groups and parties. As Oliver MacDonagh writes of O'Connell: 'he was perhaps the greatest innovator in modern democratic politics as well as the originator of almost all the basic strategies of Anglo-Irish constitutional relations'.

One other aspect of his work is of vital importance. O'Connell was undoubtedly a great national leader, and he persistently claimed to speak for all the Irish people. But his origins and background, his rapport with the Irish Catholic masses and their priests, the message and appeal of the great Associations he led, and his support for the leaders of the Irish Catholic Church on major issues, as well as the unremitting hostility of Irish Protestantism – all these made him inevitably a great national *Catholic* leader. As Oliver MacDonagh writes: 'he was in part the faithful reflector and in part the actual shaper of the emergent Irish nationalist Catholic culture'. As a result, O'Connell's career helped unwittingly to divide rather than bring together the two great religious communities of Ireland.

After 1840 O'Connell's record is clearly one of failure. The collapse of the Repeal campaign after 1843, and O'Connell's impotence during the Great Famine, was followed by the eclipse of the Irish parliamentary party after his death in 1847. All this led to a certain reaction in Ireland against the Liberator's methods of peaceful agitation coupled with involvement in parliamentary politics. The year 1848, suggests one of his modern biographers, marks the end of 'the O'Connellite tradition in Irish politics ... rendered obsolete by changes in the direction, methods and ideas of the Irish nationalist movement'.

Summary Diagram

Daniel O'Connell, 1775–1847

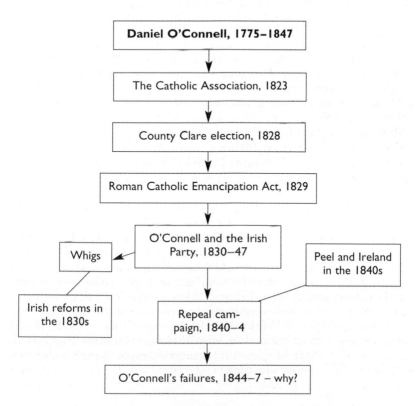

Working on Chapter 3

Full notes are required on O'Connell's career. There is a mass of detail in this chapter, hence it is essential to organise your points clearly and cogently. The best approach is probably to consider O'Connell from two points of view: his achievements and his failures. Each section should list the reasons for success or failure. A final section should attempt a summing-up of his career, and in particular consider the question 'Why is O'Connell regarded as such an outstanding figure in Anglo-Irish history?'

Answering structured and essay questions on Chapter 3

A typical structured question on O'Donnell is as follows:

I **a)** Describe the tactics O'Donnell used to achieve Catholic Emancipation.
  b) What reforms did the Whigs enact, with O'Connell's support, in the 1830s?
  c) What criticism of O'Connell were made by the leaders of 'Young Ireland' in the 1840s?
  d) What were O'Connell's major successes and failures?

Notice the way in which the final part of the question builds upon the earlier parts. But note also that you have to bring in extra factual information, for instance from the Repeal campaign, and that you have to be more evaluative here, comparing achievements and giving your assessment of them. Often a mark scheme will show the relative importance of the different parts of a stepped or structured question, and you should use this to allocate your time effectively.

A typical A level question on Daniel O'Connell is:

2 Why is Daniel O'Connell considered to be a great Irish nationalist leader?

The essence of a good answer to such a question is to achieve clarity and balance. The heart of the answer would be an analysis of O'Connell's work as a nationalist leader – which should cover his personality and aims, the methods he adopted and his achievements. The question takes for granted O'Connell's greatness. This does not mean that he was always successful: indeed, his reactions to failure might be one part of his 'greatness'. This is a point worth considering now and in later, similar questions.

Many questions on Anglo-Irish affairs cover long periods, rather than dealing with individuals or limited topics. You must be prepared to deal with this type of question. A good example of such a question on the period covered by Chapters 2 and 3 is:

3 How successfully did English politicians deal with Irish problems 1798–1843?

The topics to be dealt with in this question are fairly obvious, given the specific dates mentioned. But note once again the use of the word 'successfully'. Draw a distinction between immediate and long-term success. This is worth thinking about, as it is especially relevant to any study of 'the Irish question'.

Source-based questions on Chapter 3

1 The Repeal Campaign in the 1840s
Read the quotations from O'Connell's speech and look at the cartoon on page 43, and answer the following questions.

a) How did O'Connell propose to get 'Ireland for the Irish'? (*6 marks*)
b) 'I want you to do nothing that is not open and legal'. Why was it so difficult for O'Connell to achieve this ideal during the Repeal campaign? (*5 marks*)
c) 'There was no pursuit of Roman Catholic interests as opposed to Protestant...' Why were Irish Protestants sceptical about this claim of O'Connell's? (*4 marks*)
d) Comment briefly on the style and character of O'Connell's oratory as revealed by this passage. (*6 marks*)
e) What point is being made in the cartoon about O'Connell's position as an Irish nationalist leader? (*4 marks*)
f) How justified was the cartoon's depiction of O'Connell? (*5 marks*)

# The Great Famine

The Great Famine of 1845–9 is often seen as a great turning point in Irish history. Certainly its consequences were profound, socially, economically and politically. You have to decide what caused the Famine, whether more could have been done to mitigate its consequences and, above all, what effects it had on the Irish Question, i.e. the relationship between Britain and Ireland.

KEY DATES

1845 (September) beginning of potato blight
1846 (July) repeal of the Corn Laws; Peel replaced as PM by Lord John Russell
1847 soup-kitchens provided relief
1848 Poor Law used as means of relief; (July) Young Ireland rebellion failed
1849 better conditions returned; Encumbered Estates Act, facilitating sale of estates
1850 Irish Tenant League founded

What became known as 'the Great Famine' in Irish history began quite unexpectedly in the late summer of 1845. That summer had been a fine, warm one, and reports from the west of Ireland spoke of potato crops of 'the most luxuriant character ... promising abundant yield'. But once the potatoes began to be harvested, it soon became apparent that they were hopelessly diseased and unfit for consumption by either man or beast. Contemporaries were bewildered. By early 1846 the blight had spread to most parts of Ireland and about three-quarters of the country's potato crop was wiped out. Since the potato was the staple food of Ireland, millions were now haunted by the prospect of widespread famine. Sir Robert Peel, the Conservative Prime Minister, took remedial measures to prevent this (see pages 55–56); but though there were no deaths from starvation during his administration, there was widespread hunger among the peasantry, soon accompanied by the spread of fever, mainly typhus. It seemed apparent that unless there was a better potato harvest in the following year, or alternative supplies of cheap food became available, the Irish people faced massive starvation and death.

Hopes that the next harvest would be unaffected by the potato blight proved unfounded. One parish priest wrote early in August 1846,

1 On the 27th of last month I passed from Cork to Dublin, and this
  doomed plant bloomed in all the luxuriance of an abundant harvest.
  Returning on the 3rd of August, I beheld with sorrow one wide waste
  of putrefying vegetation. In many places the wretched people were
5 seated on the fences of their decaying gardens, wringing their hands,
  and wailing bitterly the destruction that had left them foodless.

The situation was similar throughout the whole of Ireland, and, weakened by earlier deprivation and with all their resources used up during the previous year of hunger, the Irish peasantry faced a grim winter in 1846–7. Despite the varied package of relief measures (see pages 57–60) introduced by the new Whig Prime Minister, Lord John Russell, thousands soon succumbed to starvation and disease. Others determined to leave Ireland at any cost, and the great tide of emigration across the Atlantic became a flood (see page 64). The potato harvest in 1847, though free from blight, was small and had little effect on the general situation. In 1848 the blight returned in full force, and that year proved to be one of the worst in terms of death and distress during the whole history of the Great Famine. It was not until the end of 1849 that the disappearance of the potato blight, together with improved food supplies and the total effect of the relief measures, brought the Great Famine to an end.

1 Background and Causes

> **KEY ISSUE** How did the land system serve to make life precarious for so many in Ireland?

Ireland had suffered famine earlier, notably in 1817 and 1822. What was remarkable about the Great Famine was its extent and intensity. This time it affected the whole country over four years, with profound long-term consequences for the Irish people. The immediate cause of the Famine – as we now know – was a fungal disease which attacked the potato crop. This was a disaster which was unexpected, especially since famine had disappeared from England and Scotland, and, as far as its real causes were concerned, bewildering to contemporaries. But the wider origins and character of the Great Famine were directly related to the structure of Irish social and economic life, and especially its land system. As the Devon Royal Commission reported in 1845, shortly before the outbreak of the Famine: 'the source of all Ireland's misfortunes and poverty was the fatal system of land tenure existing in the country'.

As we saw in Chapter 2, the general character of the Irish land system had been shaped by the confiscations of earlier centuries, which led to the bulk of the cultivated land falling into the hands of a small class of Protestant landowners. Some of the original estates were still held virtually intact by great aristocrats, whose agents ran them on their behalf. But over the years most of these estates had been carved up into smaller units and were leased out to middlemen on long leases at fixed rents. This new class of landowners had in turn divided up their estates into smaller farms, and they often charged high rents and lived as absentees in England. The process of division and sub-division accelerated even further in the later eighteenth and early nineteenth centuries, until by the eve of the Great Famine 24 per cent of holdings were between one and five acres (rented by the cottiers); 40 per cent were between five and 15 acres; and only about seven per cent were over 30 acres. At the very bottom of the rural scale were the million or so 'landless' labourers who worked for the farmers – when they could get work. This was not very easy when many farms were so small and labour was so plentiful, and many labourers were forced to become migratory workers to England for part of the year. Under-employment was one of the great social evils of rural Ireland. Even the domestic work of spinning and weaving, with which many smallholders and labourers had eked out their livelihood in earlier years, was now drying up as a result of the decline of the Irish woollen and domestic linen industries in the early nineteenth century. Unlike the English farm labourers, the Irish labourers were not usually paid wholly in wages but were also rewarded with scraps of land, on which they could just exist by relying on the potato. The labourers were thus virtually indistinguishable from the cottiers. It was the tiny size of peasant holdings that was therefore the characteristic feature of the Irish rural scene. Why was this?

One major cause was the dramatic rise in Irish population. Irish population was roughly 5 million in 1780 and reached about 8 millions in 1845, despite the fact that 1.5 million Irishmen emigrated to North America in the generation following the Act of Union. This population explosion was primarily due to early marriage and a very high birth rate, and probably to the general improvement in health and diet that occurred in the relatively prosperous years of the later eighteenth century. This prosperity was the result of high prices for Irish agricultural produce in England (where population was also increasing rapidly). In a country such as Ireland with virtually no industry outside Ulster, and where the overwhelming majority of the people were dependent on agriculture, such an upsurge in population growth was bound to lead to intense competition for land, even at the high rents that then prevailed. Possession of a plot of land became literally the difference between life and death. Fathers who themselves rented smallholdings were prepared to sub-divide them further in order to help their families. 'A parent must provide for his children in some way', as one tenant-farmer said, 'and he cannot send them all the way to America'.

What both encouraged sub-division and made it economically feas-
ible was the spread of the potato as the staple crop. The potato had
enormous advantages for the Irish peasant. It was easy to grow
(though impossible to store for long) and could flourish on poorish
soil. Above all, it was an economical and nutritious crop which produced high yields: one-and-a-half acres of land could provide food for
a year for a family of five or six. It could also be used to feed a pig and
poultry. Subsistence on the potato also enabled the peasantry,
especially in the more prosperous east, to concentrate on cash crops
– wheat, oats, flax, dairy produce – to pay their rent, while for the
larger farmers the provision of a tiny plot for potatoes provided a
cheap way of paying their labourers.

Thus population and the potato advanced together. On the eve of
the Famine about two million acres (one-third of the cultivated land)
was used for potatoes and provided food for some three million
people. It was in the west particularly, where plots were smallest, that
there was the greatest dependence on the potato and the grimmest
poverty. There the peasants' normal diet consisted of 12 to 14 pounds
of potatoes daily, together with a little buttermilk and oatmeal.
Conditions for these tenants – and even more so for the landless
labourers – were particularly wretched.

Basic and monotonous as their normal diet was, conditions were
even worse during the notorious 'hungry months' of the summer at
the end of the old season of potatoes and before the new had been
harvested. Then many of the peasantry existed in a state of semi-star-
vation, lacking the money to buy food and being forced to obtain
meal on credit. It was this large class of cottiers and labourers, living
on the very edge of existence, who were particularly vulnerable to any
sudden deterioration in the state of the potato crop.

2 The Response of the British Government

> **KEY ISSUE** Why did the British not do more to combat the
> famine?

a) Sir Robert Peel

Reports of the partial failure of the potato crop came to the attention
of the British government in September 1845. It gave Sir Robert Peel,
the Conservative Prime Minister, the opportunity for carrying
through the repeal of the Corn Laws (which taxed foreign grain
entering the United Kingdom), which he had believed for some time
were no longer economically defensible. To maintain the Corn Laws
while Irishmen starved would be intolerable. But, as the Prime
Minister realised, the repeal of the Corn Laws in itself could have little
effect on the situation in Ireland, given the fact that the Irish peas-

antry just could not afford to buy grain and that supplies from Europe were in any case limited. Hence, at the same time he also acted quickly to introduce relief measures to stave off potential famine in Ireland.

The government began by spending £100,000 on a supply of Indian corn (maize) from America, which was sold cheaply and so kept down the price of other grains. His main effort, however, was devoted to encouraging the Irish landlords to organise local committees to raise money for the relief of the distressed, and to provide more work on their estates. 'Our main reliance', he said, 'must be placed on the co-operation of the landed interest with local aid'. In similar fashion the Irish Board of Works, with the aid of Treasury grants, began to employ men to work on such undertakings as road repairs and road building. Peel's measures were successful in fulfilling their immediate purpose of preventing exceptional hardship during the months between the autumn of 1845 and the summer of 1846. Even the nationalist newspaper, *The Freeman's Journal*, was prepared to give the Prime Minister his due. 'The limited distress which Sir Robert Peel was called upon to meet', it wrote, 'he provided for fairly and fully. No man died of famine during his administration.'

Yet the same claim could not be made for Peel's successors. In August 1846 the potato blight struck again on a wider scale and in more virulent fashion, and the peasantry were even less prepared than earlier since their reserves had now been used up. Millions faced starvation. By that time Peel was out of power. He had successfully pushed through the repeal of the Corn Laws – in the teeth of opposition from the majority of his backbenchers. But he was shortly afterwards defeated over his proposal for a new Irish Coercion Act – which he believed was necessary to deal with potential food riots – by a 'blackguard combination' (as Wellington termed it) of all the opposition groups in the House of Commons together with the anti-Repeal Conservatives. As a result the Whigs came into power. It was Lord John Russell, therefore, who now became Prime Minister and found himself facing the grim prospect of massive famine and death in Ireland.

b) Lord John Russell

i) Government Attitudes

No reputable historian now accepts the view of the extreme nationalists, expressed at the time, that the aim of the British government was to ensure that a people 'which once numbered nine million may be checked in its growth and coolly, gradually murdered'. Yet the impatience and prejudice of English politicians and their ignorance of Irish conditions did lead some of them to blame the Irish themselves for their troubles. 'The real difficulty', wrote the newly-appointed Lord-Lieutenant, Lord Clarendon, in May 1847, 'lies with the people

themselves – they are always in the mud ... their idleness and help-
lessness can hardly be believed'. Nor were many Englishmen prepared to accept the logic of those Irishmen who argued that the
existence of the Union meant that the whole of the United Kingdom
– and not just Ireland – should accept responsibility for the Great
Famine. For most of them, including the Prime Minister, it was the
Irish landlord class who should bear the main burden.

An even greater impediment to vigorous action by the English governing caste was its almost total commitment to the principles of *lais-
sez-faire*. This meant that there must be no fundamental interference
with market conditions and the price mechanism as the main instru-
ments for providing food for the people of Ireland. Thus, in order
not to undermine the interests of traders and retailers, food must not
be provided freely or below market prices. 'It must be thoroughly
understood', announced Lord John Russell on assuming office, 'that
we cannot feed the people'. In the same way public works had to be
of general utility and were not to benefit particular individuals or
interests. In this outlook Lord John was strongly supported by his
Chancellor of the Exchequer and even more assiduously and dog-
matically by Charles Trevelyan, the Treasury official primarily responsible for the organisation of famine relief. Though an upright and
hard-working official, Trevelyan's addiction to red tape and his
unswerving commitment to 'the operation of natural causes' (his own
pet phrase) has made him the evil genius of the Great Famine for a
number of modern historians.

For all these reasons, though Lord John Russell was genuinely
moved by Irish suffering, the measures that were introduced in the
early autumn of 1846 were haphazard and limited. As the Prime
Minister indicated to the Lord-Lieutenant at this time,

1   In some cases a public work of utility may afford relief; in others you
can only order work as a test of destitution in the same way that outdoor relief is given here in time of distress ... The wages given for work
should not be unreasonable either way. It must be remembered that
5   the wages hitherto given by farmers were in addition to the stock of
potatoes grown by the cottier; now he must subsist on wages alone.
You should have a sufficiency of troops and police in any county that
seems growing into disturbance ... The priests will, I feel confident, do
all in their power to induce the people to be tranquil. You should make
10 more use of the Poor Law than was done last year. The workhouses
should be full when out-door relief is given.

ii) Relief Measures

The public works system was extended, and labourers were to be paid
less than subsistence level wages to work on unproductive tasks on
roads and bridges. By the spring of 1847 about three-quarters of a million men were employed on such schemes. In addition, by a special

'Labour Rate' Act, the screw was to be tightened on landlords to provide work or pay a 'labour rate' – a burden which many of them resented and found onerous. The demands by both landlords and nationalists for real productive work to be provided – for instance land reclamation and railway construction – were brushed by Charles Trevelyan in typical fashion. 'For the government to undertake by its own direct agency the detailed drainage and improvements of the whole country, is a task for which the nature and functions of government are totally unsuited.'

The measures taken by the government to avert famine proved to be hopelessly inadequate. It is true that, in response to high prices, grain flooded into the country and offset the food exports that had continued since the early days of the Famine. But the wages paid to the labourers under private or public schemes were insufficient to enable them to afford the rocketing prices of the imported wheat and flour. As the radical land reformer, Jeremiah O'Donovan Rossa, later wrote,

 1   The landlords made a raid upon the grain crops and sold them for their
     rents, leaving the producers of those crops to starve or perish or fly
     the country ... People now allude to those years as the 'famine' in
     Ireland; there is no famine in any country that will produce in any one
 5   year as much food as will feed the people who live in that country ...
     There was no famine, but plunder of the Irish people by the English government of Ireland.

The winter of 1846–7 was therefore grim for the peasantry. The first deaths from starvation were now reported, and in the wake of famine came disease. The limited number of hospitals and dispensaries were unable to cope. Fever was spread throughout Ireland as the stricken peasantry in the west moved into eastern rural areas and then poured into the towns. An eye-witness from Cork described how 'Crowds of starving creatures flock in from the rural districts and take possession of some hall-door or the outside of some public building where they place a little straw and remain until they die. Disease has in consequence spread itself through the town'.

By January 1847 even Trevelyan appeared to recognise the extent of the government's failure. 'The tide of distress', he wrote to a colleague, 'has for some time been steadily rising and appears now to have completely overflowed the barriers we endeavoured to oppose to it'. Lord John Russell therefore abruptly changed his policy.

In the spring of 1847 the public works projects and the labour rate were abandoned, and the government now pinned its hopes for relief on direct help – free distribution of food via soup-kitchens. However, this was to be funded through the local rates, though the government was prepared to advance money to the local authorities which was to be repaid later. By August over three million people were being fed in this way, though, of course, the scheme came too late to help the many who had already died of hunger or disease. Food was also provided by private charity and voluntary organisations, especially by the Quakers, who did magnificent work in the stricken west of Ireland. But since the government had always insisted that the free distribution of food was a temporary measure, and the harvest of late summer and autumn in 1847 was a good one, the soup-kitchen system was brought to an end, with little warning, in September of that year.

The government now decided to provide relief entirely through a reorganised Poor Law system, which was to be made available to all those who were suffering directly from the Famine. As a result about 200,000 of the ill, hungry and destitute were accepted into the workhouses – though those who possessed more than a quarter-acre of land were refused entry. Since the workhouses had been designed to cope with only about half that number, the conditions in them were appalling and disease spread rapidly. In 1847 there were 130 deaths in the Limerick workhouse alone. Moreover, since relief was to be financed almost totally out of the Irish poor law rates – though, as with earlier schemes, the Treasury provided some help – many Poor Law Unions were soon bankrupt. As the *Cork Examiner* had written prophetically in 1846: 'We should not wonder if these workhouses became the charnel houses of the whole rural population.'

In the end, owing to the obvious inability of the workhouses themselves to cope with the demands made upon them, a system of 'outdoor relief' was introduced, and in this way about 800,000 victims of the Famine were given relief in their own homes.

It was this system of workhouse and outdoor relief that was expected to deal with the consequences of the final disastrous potato harvest in 1848 and its aftermath, until better conditions returned at the end of 1849. In effect, Ireland was thus left to her fate. 'I do not think that any effort of this house', Lord John Russell told the Commons in May 1849, 'would, in the present and unfortunate state of Ireland, be capable of preventing the dreadful scenes of suffering and death that are now occurring in Ireland'.

The operation of the Irish Poor Law system during the later years of the Famine had one other indirect consequence. The burden of paying the local poor rate was particularly onerous for a number of landlords and farmers, since it was proportionate to the number of tenants on their land; and this fact, together with the difficulties in collecting rent, led some of them to evict their tenants and turn the land over to pastoral farming. This trend was accentuated by some small-holders voluntarily giving up their land in order to obtain poor relief. Eviction in the midst of starvation produced some of the most heartrending scenes during the whole history of the Great Famine, and desperation sometimes led to violence and intimidation and to isolated cases of landlords being murdered. On the other hand, it is only fair to point out that evictions were not on an abnormally large scale during this period; indeed one historian of the Famine concludes that they were 'the exception rather than the rule'.

The Treasury spent a total of about £8 million on Irish relief, much of it in the form of loans to the Irish Board of Works or Poor Law authorities. About half of the loans had not been repaid by 1850, and the money was written off by the Treasury three years later. The British government congratulated itself on what it had done financially for Irish relief – and Trevelyan wrote, characteristically, that 'too much has been done for the people'; yet Ireland spent considerably more than £8 millions on its own relief if we add together the rates collected by the various Irish agencies and private contributions from landlords and others. One authority has argued that British government relief expenditure was in fact small in relation to its resources, amounting to no more than 2–3 per cent of public expenditure in the 1840s. Other historians, however, have stressed the difficulties that would have faced any government dealing with famine conditions in Ireland at this time: lack of good communications, a primitive system of retail distribution, an ineffective system of local government, and wide social, regional and religious differences. They have therefore adopted a more sympathetic attitude towards the efforts of Peel and Russell.

3 The Results of the Great Famine

> **KEY ISSUES** What were the economic and demographic effects of the famine? Why was there not a greater political backlash against the Union?

a) Population and Land

The most dramatic consequence of the Great Famine was on the population of Ireland. About one million Irish men, women and children died between 1845 and 1850 as a result of starvation and disease, and a further one-and-a-half million emigrated. Hence the Irish population declined by about a quarter during this period: from roughly eight millions (according to the 1841 census) to about six millions (according to the 1851 census). Furthermore, the decline continued. This was mainly due to a reduction in the birth rate owing to later and fewer marriages in the post-Famine epoch, and the continuation of emigration. As a result the Irish population in 1900 was about half what it had been in 1845.

Inevitably, these demographic changes had a powerful impact on the pattern of landholding. The cottier class of smallholders was almost completely wiped out as a result of death or emigration. This encouraged the consolidation of holdings, with the cottiers' plots being taken over by the larger farmers, many of whom had survived the Famine in reasonable circumstances. In this way about 200,000 smallholdings – one farm out of every four – disappeared. Thus, whereas before 1845 only just over one-third of farms were over 15 acres in size, by 1851 about one-half were.

At the other end of the social scale, members of the old landlord class were also badly affected economically by the Famine. This was the result of the extra financial burdens imposed on them by labour and poor rates – often on top of mortgages and debts – at a time when it was obviously difficult to collect rents. About ten per cent of landlords went bankrupt. For legal reasons, they often found it difficult to dispose of their estates easily. As a result, the Whig government passed the Encumbered Estates Act of 1849 to speed up the sale of land, hoping, in addition, that this would lead to the emergence of a new, more enterprising landlord class, prepared to invest money in their estates. In this way about 3,000 estates were sold in the 1850s, amounting to about 5 million acres. But in fact most of the new landlords turned out to be either speculators, who raised rents to extortionate heights (rack-renting), or those members of the old landlord class who had survived the recent crisis with enough spare capital to buy up cheaply the estates now thrown on the market.

The aftermath of the Great Famine also saw the emergence of a more balanced farming system with less concentration on tillage, and especially potato cultivation, and more on pastoral farming. The move to pastoral farming which had been discernible after 1815 (as a result of the general slump in grain prices) increased considerably after 1850, especially in the form of dairy farming and the export of live cattle. By 1870 the acreage devoted to grain and potatoes had halved compared with pre-Famine days, though the potato still remained an important food staple in the west of Ireland, where the old rural economy changed extremely slowly. During these years too farmers and landlords expanded the area of cultivation by well over a million acres, a development which vividly reveals how much useful, productive work could have been carried out in pre-Famine Ireland.

The decline in population, by reducing the pressure on resources in Ireland, also led to a rise in average living standards. Labourers' wages rose – helped by a considerable drop in their numbers from 1.2 millions (1845) to 0.7 millions (1861). Housing standards improved – the old one-room cabin began to disappear in the countryside – and, in the aftermath of the Famine, Ireland became a more literate and a more urbanised society. This was the result of the building of more schools, and the growth of Irish towns at the expense of the countryside; and both of these developments were signs of the relative prosperity of Ireland in third quarter of the nineteenth century.

What all these changes in landownership and farming practice meant was that the medium-sized (by Irish standards) family farm of five to 30 acres, devoted to mixed farming, became the norm. It was this middle-class farming group, many of whom had done relatively well during the Famine years, who now became the key group in the Irish countryside. Their domination was encouraged by their continuing prosperity as a result of the expansion of Irish agriculture, especially pastoral farming, during the years between the 1850s and the 1870s, when farmers' income rose by about 77 per cent. It was helped also by the 1850 Reform Act which, by enlarging the Irish county electorate, gave many of these farmers the vote. Thus, in the aftermath of the Great Famine and the fiasco of the 1848 rebellion (which is discussed in the next section), the farmers' demands over land became the most important theme in Irish politics in the 1850s.

b) Irish Nationalism and Politics

The failure of Daniel O'Connell's Repeal campaign and the death of the Liberator himself in 1847 paved the way for the emergence of a more extreme group of Irish nationalists associated with the 'Young Ireland' movement. Under the influence of the Great Famine – for which they held the British government responsible – they began to toy with the idea of armed rebellion. The key figure here was John Mitchel, the son of a Presbyterian minister. In 1847 he formed his own newspaper, *United Irishmen*, to espouse his views, aided, notably, by Fintan Lalor, Gavan Duffy, William Smith O'Brien and James Dillon, all of whom were middle-class literary and professional men. Mitchel's political views were summed up in his notorious cry – which links him with the rebels of 1798 and echoes down the years – 'Give us war in our time, O Lord'. He argued that 'legal and constitutional agitation in Ireland, is a delusion ... every man ought to have arms and to promote their use'; and he called for a war of vengeance against England in order to achieve 'an Irish Republic, one and indivisible'.

Mitchel was also influenced by the important writings of his colleague Fintan Lalor on the land question. Lalor wanted to sweep away the landlord system on the grounds that, morally, the land belonged to the Irish people, and replace it with a nation of independent peasant proprietors. The Irish people's 'full right of ownership' over their land 'ought to be asserted and enforced by any and all reasons which God has put into the power of man'. A truly independent Ireland, Lalor argued, could only be achieved on the basis of a free peasantry.

The move towards rebellion in Ireland was encouraged by the contemporary Chartist movement in Britain and, even more, by the outbreak of revolution in Paris in February 1848. 'We must resist, we must act ... if needs be we must die, rather than let this providential hour pass over us unliberated', proclaimed Gavan Duffy. It was the British government, however, which acted first. In May Mitchel was arrested, condemned on a charge of treason, and transported for 14 years. Nevertheless, his followers began an abortive rebellion in

Ireland in July 1848. It was a hopeless affair from the start. It was badly led and badly organised; there was no mass support from a half-starved and demoralised peasantry; and the Roman Catholic Church was against it. The Irish rebellion of 1848 ended within a few weeks in a tragi-comic affray between a handful of peasants led by the Young Irelanders, and the police, at a remote farm house – 'the battle of the Widow McCormack's cabbage patch', as it is derisively known. It was followed by the subsequent arrest of the leaders. Dillon escaped, but O'Brien was tried and transported.

'The rebellion', writes the historian F.S.L. Lyons, 'exhibited all the classical symptoms of romantic idealism totally out of touch with the world of reality'. Nevertheless, he suggests that the 'men of 1848' bequeathed at least two important ideas to their nationalist successors. First, the ideal of an independent Irish Republic, to be fought for and if necessary died for. Secondly, the notion of a land war of tenants versus landlords as a fundamental part of this process of liberation – as discussed and justified in Lalor's writings on the Irish land system. This became a grim reality in Ireland in the 1870s.

But these were long-term results, and emphasis on 'Young Ireland' gives a false picture of the reality of politics in the aftermath of the Great Famine. For during the 1850s Ireland largely succumbed to political apathy; and, for the middle-class farmers at least, this expressed itself in a concern with their immediate social and economic interests rather than the more abstract doctrines of nationalism. Hence their support for the tenant-right movement.

Irish tenant leagues emerged at the end of the Great Famine on a local basis, partly in response to the evictions that were being carried out by some landlords, but also as an expression of the new power of the larger farmers based on their now dominant social, economic and political position in rural Ireland. The leagues demanded 'tenant right': that is, fair rents and compensation from the landlords for improvements carried out by the tenants if they were evicted. The Whig government had promised some reform in this direction, but in the end nothing was done. The local groups combined together to form an All-Ireland Tenant League in 1850; and they were supported (after the general election of 1852) by a small group of Irish MPs of all political persuasions, calling themselves the 'Independent Irish Party'. But not even the ideal of 'tenant right' was strong enough to overcome social and religious differences, particularly between Ulster Protestants and the rest of Ireland; and this, together with the general political apathy of the time and a temporary slump in farming prices in 1859, led to the collapse of the tenants' movement at the end of the 1850s. Nevertheless, it did succeed in making 'tenant right' an important part of any future Irish reform programme.

For similar reasons the Independent Irish Party disintegrated about the same time. It is notable that in the general election of 1859 the Conservative Party actually won a majority of Irish seats (55 out of

105), a result which is linked with the hardening of unionist senti-
ment in Ulster, and one historian sees this as evidence of something
like a 'Conservative revival' in Irish politics in the post-Famine period.
Certainly, no great Irish national movement emerged during the
years immediately following the Great Famine, and the political status
quo in Ireland remained relatively undisturbed until the rise of the
Irish Home Rule Party in the later 1870s, which is discussed in the
next chapter.

c) Emigration

'Emigration', writes Roy Foster, 'is the great fact of Irish social history
from the early nineteenth century'. The figures certainly bear this
out. Between 1815 and 1845 about 1.5 million Irish people emigrated;
about the same number left Ireland between 1845 and 1850, the
period of the Great Famine; another 4.5 to 5 million people emigrated during the period 1850–1910. About a quarter of these emigrants went to England and Scotland, where industrialisation
provided plenty of work and where settled Irish communities had
existed since the early eighteenth century; but the majority of them
went overseas, principally to the United States.

Despite the impression of continuity given by these emigration figures, there were important differences between the character of Irish
emigration before, and during and after the period of the Great
Famine. For most Irish families before 1845 the prospect of emigration was not something to be welcomed. The ties of kinship, locality
and land were still powerful enough to overcome the sound, practical
reasons for leaving a poverty-stricken, over-populated island to settle
in countries overseas with more abundant opportunities. Those who
did emigrate in the eighteenth and early nineteenth centuries were
generally single, landless young men, mainly from Ulster, who were
well enough off to be able to afford the fare to the New World.

During the Great Famine, however, the motivation and pattern of
emigration changed. The key year here is 1847 when, following the
disasters of that winter, something like 'panic and hysteria' gripped
many Irish families, especially the cottiers and labourers, and led to a
mass flight from Ireland. 'All we want', said one of them, 'is to get out
of Ireland . . . we must be better anywhere than here'. Hence, whereas
in 1846 106,000 emigrated, the figure for 1847 leapt to 230,000, and
most of these emigrants went to Canada and the United States. The
events of 1847, contends Oliver MacDonagh, 'by relaxing the peasants' desperate hold upon his land and home . . . destroyed the
psychological barrier which had forbidden his going so long'. It therefore made mass emigration a real, acceptable alternative. The emigration figure for 1848 was about the same as for 1847; between 1849
and 1852 about 200,000 left Ireland annually; and in 1851 – another
key year – some 250,000 emigrants left for North America alone.

In the earlier years of the Famine, though the majority of emigrants were from the poorest groups, some were from higher up the social scale. Their departure from Ireland was a rational response to what one Irish MP in 1849 described as 'a ruined proprietary, a fugitive tenantry, a destitute people, and a desolate land'. For even the better-off farmers were faced with the consequences of higher rates and taxes, the decline of commerce, the disintegration of social life, and, above all, the loss of hope for the future. After 1850, however, it

The Causes of Emigration from Ireland – *The Lady's Newspaper,* 1849

was the smallholders and labourers who were mainly responsible for the high emigration figures. Thus in all about two millions left Ireland during the decade 1845 to 1855. It was now whole families rather than individuals who departed; the very poor predominated; and, though all parts of Ireland were represented among the emigrants, the majority now came from the poverty-stricken south and south-west, rather than, as earlier, Ulster and the north.

However, emigration was no easy option. It is true that the cost of passage across the Atlantic was relatively cheap by modern standards, varying between two to five pounds according to the port of arrival. Even so it was too much for some potential emigrants; and a number were assisted by their landlords – anxious to clear their estates of smallholders – or borrowed the money, or obtained remittances or pre-paid tickets from friends or relations who were already resident in the New World. Virtually nothing was done by the British government itself to sponsor emigration.

For many emigrants the 40-day journey across the Atlantic was almost as hazardous as famine conditions in Ireland itself, and they were exploited unmercifully. Many of the ships – the notorious 'coffin ships' – were barely seaworthy, and conditions aboard were primitive in the extreme. About 20 per cent of emigrants perished on board or soon after landing. One monument to the dead at Grosse Isle in Canada, put up by their descendants, reads,

i Thousands of the children of the Gael were lost on this island while fleeing from foreign tyrannical laws and an artificial famine in the years 1847–8. God bless them. God save Ireland!

It was this hatred of England, based in part on the above view of the Great Famine, that most Irish emigrants took with them to the New World. With the rise of a large and politically influential Irish community in the United States in the second half of the nineteenth century – linked in all sorts of ways with the 'Old Country' – these perceptions were bound to influence the history of the Irish question. It is no coincidence, then, that the Fenian movement – the most important Irish revolutionary group in the 1860s – emerged out of and gained some of its most fervent recruits within the American Irish community. It is the Fenian outrages in England in 1867 that form part of the background to Gladstone's adoption of his mission 'to pacify Ireland' – the major theme of the next chapter.

Summary Diagram

The Great Famine

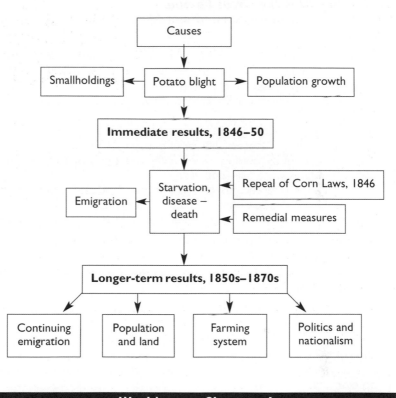

```
                    ┌─────────────┐
                    │   Causes    │
                    └──────┬──────┘
                           ▼
┌──────────────┐   ┌──────────────┐   ┌──────────────────┐
│ Smallholdings │◄─│ Potato blight │─►│ Population growth │
└──────────────┘   └──────┬───────┘   └──────────────────┘
                          ▼
              ┌───────────────────────────┐
              │ Immediate results, 1846–50 │
              └─────────────┬─────────────┘
                            ▼
                    ┌──────────────┐   ┌──────────────────────────┐
                    │  Starvation, │◄──│ Repeal of Corn Laws, 1846 │
┌────────────┐     │  disease –   │   └──────────────────────────┘
│ Emigration │◄────│   death      │   ┌──────────────────┐
└────────────┘     │              │◄──│ Remedial measures │
                    └──────┬───────┘   └──────────────────┘
                           ▼
              ┌─────────────────────────────────┐
              │ Longer-term results, 1850s–1870s │
              └────┬──────────┬──────────┬───────┘
                   ▼          ▼          ▼          ▼
          ┌───────────┐ ┌──────────┐ ┌─────────┐ ┌──────────────┐
          │Continuing │ │Population│ │ Farming │ │ Politics and │
          │emigration │ │ and land │ │ system  │ │ nationalism  │
          └───────────┘ └──────────┘ └─────────┘ └──────────────┘
```

Working on Chapter 4

After considering the causes and immediate impact of the Great Famine on the Irish people, you should compile a fairly detailed account of the British government's response. This is complicated, so try not to get bogged down in too much detail. Concentrate on general questions in your notes: what were the aims of the government? what methods of relief did they adopt and why? how successful were they? As far as the longer-term results of the Famine are concerned, work out and list those which are directly or indirectly related to the Irish question.

Source-based questions on Chapter 4

1 The Impact of the Great Famine
Read the extracts on pages 53, 57 and 58, and answer the following questions.

a) What caused the potato to become 'the doomed plant' in 1846? What were the immediate results of this for the Irish peasants? (*6 marks*)
b) The priest's Diary says the peasants were left 'foodless'. Rossa says, 'There was no famine in Ireland'. How do you explain this contradiction? (*5 marks*)
c) What were the 'public works' referred to by Lord John Russell? Why were they not very successful as relief measures? (*5 marks*)
d) What was meant by 'outdoor relief'? Why was it only be to given when the workhouses were full? (*6 marks*)
e) What does the reference to 'troops and police' indicate about the attitude of the authorities during the Famine? (*3 marks*)
f) Use these sources and other information to explain why more was not done to tackle the Famine. (*10 marks*)

2 Emigration
Look at the cartoon on page 65, and read the inscription on page 66, and answer the following questions.

a) In the cartoon, why is America shown as the rising sun for the emigrant? (*6 marks*)
b) What evidence in the cartoon indicates the likely social status and position of the emigrant? (*5 marks*)
c) Explain briefly three reasons shown in the cartoon which induced him to emigrate. (*6 marks*)
d) The inscription refers to 'foreign tyrannical laws and an artificial famine'. What laws are meant? And why is the famine described as 'artificial'? (*4 marks*)
e) Describe briefly one important consequence for Great Britain of Irish emigration to the United States in the nineteenth century. (*4 marks*)
f) Use these two sources and your own knowledge to explain the range of motives which led people to emigrate. (*10 marks*)

5 Gladstone and Irish Reform, 1868–82

POINTS TO CONSIDER

The period 1868–82 is of immense significance in the history of the Irish Question. You need to understand the policies pursued by Gladstone's governments, particularly on the issue of land; the growth of Irish nationalism, under men like Butt, Davitt and Parnell; and the reasons for the extensive violence that broke out, particularly in 1879–82. But be certain to keep in mind important two overall questions. First, whether moderate reform could possibly fulfil Irish needs and aspirations. Second, whether Irish nationalism would aim at reform within the Union or independence, using peaceful or violent tactics.

KEY DATES

1858	Irish Republican Brotherhood (Fenians) founded by James Stephens in Dublin
1867	Fenian outrages in Ireland and England
1868	(December) Liberal victory at general election; Gladstone formed his first ministry
1869	Irish Church Act
1870	Gladstone's first Irish Land Act
1873	(March) defeat of Irish Universities Bill; (November) Home Rule League founded by Isaac Butt
1874	Conservative victory at general election: 60 Home Rulers elected
1877	'Obstructionism' in the House of Commons
1879	Foundation of Irish National Land League
1880	(April) Liberal victory at general election: Gladstone's second ministry; (May) Parnell elected leader of the Irish Parliamentary Party
1881	(March) Coercion Act; (August) Gladstone's second Irish Land Act; (October) Parnell arrested, Land League outlawed
1882	(May) Kilmainham Treaty between Parnell and Gladstone; (May) Phoenix Park murders

1 Gladstone and Ireland, 1868–74

KEY ISSUE With what success did Gladstone introduce a series of reforms to remedy Irish grievances and ensure the stability of the Union?

a) Gladstone's 'Mission'

In the spring of 1866 a Liberal Reform Bill was defeated in the House of Commons, leading to the resignation of the government. Lord Derby and Disraeli then came into power at the head of a minority Conservative administration, and it was they who pushed through a Reform Bill in the summer of 1867. The Conservative Bill was, ironically, a much more democratic measure than the original Liberal proposal – which aimed to enfranchise only a small minority of the urban working class – since it was based upon the principle of 'household suffrage'. The Reform Act of 1867 added over a million new voters to the electorate, most of them working men who now became a majority of the voters in urban areas. About one in three adult men could now vote, as opposed to one in five previously.

The passage of the Second Reform Act was soon followed by the retirement of Earl Russell and the succession of Gladstone as Liberal leader. Early in 1868 Lord Derby also retired and Disraeli became Conservative Prime Minister for the first time. But his period of power was short-lived. In the spring of 1868 Gladstone introduced a series of resolutions into the House of Commons in favour of the disestablishment of the Church of Ireland – one of the pillars of the Protestant Ascendancy – and they were passed by comfortable majorities against the protests of the government. Opposition to religious privilege was a subject on which all Liberals could unite. The result was the dissolution of parliament and the holding of a general election in November 1868. In his election campaign Gladstone made Irish reform one of the major issues. In one of his most famous speeches, at Wigan in October, he compared the Protestant Ascendancy in Ireland with,

1   some tall tree of noxious growth, lifting its head to heaven and poisoning the atmosphere of the land so far as its shadow can extend ... But now at last the day has come when, as we hope, the axe has been laid to the root. It is deeply cut round and round. It nods and quivers from
5   top to base. There lacks but one stroke more – the stroke of these elections. It will then, once for all, topple to its fall, and on that day the heart of Ireland will leap for joy.

The result of the general election of 1868 was a triumph for Gladstone; the Liberals were swept into power with a majority of over 100. Gladstone heard the news by telegram while he was at the family estate at Hawarden Castle in North Wales, engaged in his favourite hobby of felling trees. 'Very significant', he replied, leaning on his axe, and then, turning to his companion, he uttered the famous words, 'My mission is to pacify Ireland'. Why, then, did Gladstone decide to take up the Irish question in 1868?

His action in that year was not the inevitable outcome of a long and consuming interest in Irish affairs. The famous letter he wrote to his sister in 1845 is often quoted: 'Ireland, Ireland! That cloud in the

west, that coming storm, the minister of God's retribution upon cruel
... injustice. Ireland forces upon us these great social and great religious questions'. Yet Gladstone paid little attention to that country
over the next 21 years. His one practical action was his introduction
of income tax in Ireland in 1853, during his period as Chancellor of
the Exchequer, and he made only one visit there throughout his long
life, in 1877. Nor were conditions in Ireland exceptionally bad in
1868. Farming remained prosperous, and the figures for agrarian
crime and violence were relatively low. Perhaps his renewed interest
in Ireland after 1867 was a response to the Fenian outrages of that
year.

The Fenians were members of a secret revolutionary organisation
established in Ireland (under the name of the Irish Republican
Brotherhood) and the United States in 1858, and committed to the
forcible overthrow of British power and the establishment of an independent Irish republic. (The movement drew its name from the
ancient Irish warriors, the *Fianna*.) They gained a fair amount of support in the 1860s, and even had their own newspaper, *The Irish People*,
run by the movement's Irish founder and leader, James Stephens.

In 1865 the British government responded by suppressing *The Irish
People* and arresting leading Fenians throughout Great Britain. The
Brotherhood planned an armed outbreak in Ireland early in 1867,
but this was a complete fiasco owing to the preparedness of the authorities and the lack of any widespread popular support. The Fenians
then transferred their activities to the English mainland, carrying out
two attacks which made them notorious but earned them massive
publicity. The first incident took place in September 1867 at
Manchester when, in carrying out the successful rescue of two leading
Fenians from a prison van, a policeman was killed. The second incident occurred in London in December where the terrorists blew up
part of the wall of Clerkenwell Prison in order to secure the release of
some Fenian prisoners, with the loss of about a dozen innocent lives.
In England the outrages were greeted with horror and anger. Yet in
Ireland the three Fenians who were arrested and executed for the
murder of the policeman (whose death may have been accidental)
became known as the 'Manchester Martyrs'.

Though Gladstone later denied that the Fenian activities had any
direct influence on his Irish policy, he did argue powerfully that 'they
brought home to the popular mind ... the vast importance of the
Irish controversy'. Fenianism helped to confirm his growing conviction that the Irish had genuine grievances which must be dealt with if
Ireland was to be maintained within the Union in peace and prosperity. It also made the British public, he believed, more amenable to
Irish reform. In a public speech at Southport, only a few days after the
Manchester outrage, he outlined a programme of Irish reform which
covered religion, land and university education. Nevertheless, if the
Fenian activities in 1867 help to explain the timing of Gladstone's

practical commitment to Irish reform, that commitment itself was taken up – as he insisted in a letter to his sister in 1868 – in the name of 'the God of truth and justice'. It is that principle of 'justice' that had convinced him for many years that the position of the Church of Ireland was indefensible. And it is Gladstone's concern with 'justice for Ireland' as the mainspring of his Irish policy, that is the dominant theme of J.L. Hammond's classic work, *Gladstone and the Irish Nation* (1938).

On the other hand, Gladstone was not unaware of the political advantages of Irish reform. His support for the disestablishment of the Church of Ireland in his parliamentary resolutions in the spring of 1868 may also have been conceived as a means of re-uniting the Liberal Party after the divisions over parliamentary reform in 1866–7, and also as an attempt – which turned out to be successful, as it led to the 1868 general election – to regain the political initiative from Disraeli. Moreover, Gladstone believed that with the enlarged electorate created by the Second Reform Act, Irish church reform would appeal not only to Roman Catholics but also to nonconformists and working men throughout Great Britain, many of whom were opposed to the privileges of their own Anglican churches. Gladstone declared of the electoral campaign:

> Our three [armies] – I may almost say have been Scottish Presbyterians, English and Welsh nonconformists, and Irish Roman Catholics ... The English clergy as a body have done their worst against us.

On the whole Gladstone's expectations were fulfilled. Though religion was not the only factor at work, it is significant that the Liberals improved their electoral position in Ireland (where they won 66 seats in 1868 compared with 50 in 1859), Wales and Scotland, as well as in many of the industrial areas of the north of England. However difficult it may be to pin down exactly Gladstone's motives, his actions in 1868 certainly helped to place the Irish question at the forefront of British politics.

b) Gladstone's Irish Reforms

i) The Irish Church Act 1869

The disestablishment of the Church of Ireland had played an important part in the Liberal Party's electoral campaign and was bound to be top of the new government's agenda. The case for reform was virtually unanswerable. Though the Church of Ireland had been the Established Church since the later seventeenth century, it had never represented more than a tiny minority of the Irish people. The point was driven home emphatically by the census of 1861 which showed that out of a population of 5.75 millions, the Catholics numbered 4.5 millions, and the members of the Church of Ireland less than 0.75 million. Even the Conservatives now accepted that the position of the

Church of Ireland was anomalous and required change. As Prime Minister in 1868 Disraeli had laboured, unavailingly, to find a measure of reform which, while stopping short of disestablishment, would be acceptable to all sections of his party.

Gladstone had no such inhibitions, and the Church Bill he now produced was based upon the simple principle of disestablishment and disendowment. The first part of the Bill was comparatively straightforward: the disestablishment clauses meant that the link between Church and State was to be broken and the Church of Ireland was to become a separate, voluntary organisation from 1 January 1871. This meant, for example, that tithes no longer had to be paid to the Church by all Irishmen and that Irish Anglican Archbishops and Bishops would no longer sit in the House of Lords.

The problem of disendowment – that is, the disposal of the properties belonging to the Church of Ireland – proved more difficult, since Gladstone was torn between the demands of the Anglicans (who argued that all the funds should be used to help the dispossessed members of their church), and the Catholics (who wanted most of the money to be used for secular purposes in Ireland). In the end a compromise was produced which was reasonably fair and acceptable. £10 million pounds was to be granted to the Church of Ireland for pensions to their clergy and compensation for loss of office; £13 million was to be granted for secular purposes, mainly the relief of poverty and education in Ireland.

In order to bring the other churches in Ireland into line with the new status of the Anglican Church, the state grant to the Catholic Maynooth College and the Presbyterian Church was abolished, though compensation was provided. Another significant clause in the Bill facilitated the purchase of the lands of the Church of Ireland by their tenants, and about 6,000 farmers took advantage of this, thus laying down a precedent for the future.

The Bill easily passed through the House of Commons, and the Conservative majority in the Lords was not prepared to generate a constitutional crisis by opposing it so soon after the Second Reform Act had introduced a more democratic political system. The Irish Church Act of 1869 was one of the more successful pieces of Irish legislation passed by Gladstone, since it solved once and for all the major religious grievance of the Irish Roman Catholics. Yet in practice it made little difference to the lives of the majority of the Irish people.

ii) The First Irish Land Act 1870

The subject of land reform was much more difficult than church reform owing to the complexities of the Irish land system and the wider range of interests involved, and on this subject Gladstone was forced to rely for information and advice on others. He concluded that the main problem was the landlord-tenant relationship, and that what was needed was to give more economic security to the tenant. To some extent, therefore, Gladstone was prepared to go along with the demands of the supporters of tenant right, as they had developed since the 1850s (see page 63).

The first part of Gladstone's Bill concerned those lands – mainly in the north – which were rented in accordance with what was known as 'the Ulster custom'. In these areas tenants could not be evicted so long as they continued to pay their rent. In addition, such tenants also possessed the right of 'free sale': that is, if a tenant gave up his holding, he had the right to 'sell' his interest in it to an acceptable incoming tenant by claiming compensation for the work he had put into it. Both these rights were based on 'custom' not law. What the Land Bill now proposed was that these customary rights should be given the force of law.

The second part of the Bill dealt with the problem of eviction. Tenants who were evicted were to be compensated by the landlord for the improvements they had made to their holdings, and a scale of damages was laid down. In addition, a tenant was to be compensated in similar fashion if he was evicted for any reason other than non-payment of rent. Gladstone's aim in the Land Bill was thus, as he explained, 'to prevent the landlord from using the terrible weapon of undue and unjust eviction, by so framing the handle that it shall cut his hands with the sharp edge of pecuniary damages'.

The third part of the Land Bill (known as the 'John Bright Clauses', after the Radical minister who proposed them) dealt with land purchase. It enabled a tenant wishing to purchase his holding from a landlord to obtain two-thirds of the purchase price as a grant from the state.

Gladstone's intended his Land Bill to be a one-off, distinctly Irish measure, with no implications for the rest of the United Kingdom. He did not regard it, therefore, as in any sense an attack on the rights of property. Indeed, since so much of the Bill was concerned with upholding customary rights, it could be regarded as a 'conservative' measure. Similarly, the Land Bill was meant not to undermine but to improve the position of the Irish landlord class by removing some of the obstacles to a good relationship with their tenants. What Gladstone wanted was to make Irish landlords more like English landlords: 'a position', as he said, 'marked by residence, by personal familiarity, and by sympathy with the people among whom they live'. In both respects, however, Gladstone was to some extent deluding himself, since the Land Act in the end, at least by implication, was more anti-property and anti-landlord than he admitted. In particular, the legal recognition of the right of 'free sale' implied that the tenant had an 'interest' in the land he rented which made him almost a joint owner.

Gladstone's Land Bill passed through both houses of parliament with virtually no opposition. As one English peer noted shrewdly, 'the great mass of the English people would sacrifice the Irish landlords tomorrow if they knew that by doing so they could tempt the Irish populace into acquiescing in their rule'. But the Irish Land Act was not very successful even in its own terms. The problem of defining legally where the 'Ulster custom' existed was extraordinarily complicated; and the 'Bright Clauses' too were a failure since they offered no incentive to the landlord to sell, and few tenants could afford the one-third of the purchase price needed to buy their holding. Above all, the eviction clauses had little impact since the question of controlling rents was ignored; and tenants on long leases were in any case outside the provisions of the Act. Some economic historians go further and argue that as a cure for the ills of rural Ireland the Act was almost totally irrelevant. Irish poverty was not due to the iniquity of the landlords, but to the lack of economic growth, and, in the west particularly, to the shortage of cultivable land. Rents were moderate in the 20 years following the Great Famine; evictions were few; and agricultural improvements were carried out, often jointly by landlords and tenants. 'The Land Act of 1870', it has been written, 'was the remedy for a disease that was not seriously affecting Ireland in 1870'.

Yet in a sense this argument is beside the point. As other historians have insisted, Gladstone's aims were essentially political: to bind Ireland to the Union and its institutions by proving that the Westminster parliament was prepared to legislate for what the mass of the Irish people considered to be their legitimate grievances. The Land Act therefore (in F.S.L. Lyons' phrase) 'had a symbolic significance', for, whatever its defects in strictly economic terms, it could be regarded as a further blow against the power of the Ascendancy. It was noticeable that Gladstone's reform legislation of 1869–70, together with the release of the Fenian political prisoners which he secured at the end of 1870, was followed by a new harmony between English Liberals and Irish Catholics, just as it spread alarm and despondency among Irish Protestants. All this seemed to Gladstone to justify his policies, particularly over land, and in the 1870s he remained supremely optimistic about the future of Ireland within the Union. Some politicians, however, were less starry-eyed. Lord Kimberley, the Colonial Secretary, wrote in his Journal on 21 February 1870 that no measure of any kind would satisfy the Irish: 'Gladstone now lives in the happy delusion that his policy will produce a speedy change in the temper of the Irish towards this country. He will soon find out his mistake.'

Nevertheless, Gladstone remained confident. 'There is nothing that Ireland has asked and which this country and this parliament have refused', he proclaimed in a public speech in 1871, except for the 'simple grievance' of university education. To this he now turned.

iii) The Irish Universities Bill 1873

University reform was badly needed since the Catholics of Ireland, though they controlled a number of small colleges, had no major degree-awarding institutions of their own. Trinity College, Dublin, was an Anglican foundation, and the 'godless colleges' established by Sir Robert Peel in the 1840s as non-denominational institutions were denounced by the Catholic clergy. Gladstone now proposed the establishment of a national, non-denominational University of Dublin, which would embrace both Trinity College and the present and future Catholic colleges. But the project was fraught with difficulties. Even apart from the practical problems of teaching 'controversial' subjects such as history and theology, Trinity had no wish to be involved in such an institution. But the main stumbling block proved to be the proviso that any new Catholic college would get no financial help from the state.

The Irish Universities Bill (which was made the subject of a vote of confidence) was defeated in the Commons in March 1873 by three votes because of abstentions or opposition votes by Irish Liberal MPs. Hence Gladstone resigned. But as Disraeli for purely tactical reasons refused to assume office, he soon came back into power. Nevertheless, increasing disunity and acrimony within the Parliamentary Liberal Party meant that the government's days were numbered. Moreover, in Ireland a Home Rule Party had already arisen to challenge the power of the established parties. 'The Universities Bill stated what the 1874 general election confirmed: Liberal Ireland was soon to be dead and gone.'

2 The Rise of Parnell

KEY ISSUES What factors led to the growth of the Home Rule movement in Ireland?

Even while Gladstone was promoting his Irish reforms a new movement for constitutional change in Ireland had arisen. The leading figure was Isaac Butt, an Irish Protestant lawyer. Butt had begun his political career as a staunch Unionist, and indeed sat in the House of Commons as a Conservative MP from 1852 to 1865. But his growing disillusionment with the House of Commons as a vehicle for dealing effectively with Irish affairs, together with the personal example of the Fenian political prisoners whom he defended in the courts after 1865, led him to become an Irish nationalist. He had no sympathy with the Fenian ideal of armed rebellion and Irish independence, but he now believed that some form of self-government for Ireland, based on an elected Irish Parliament to deal with domestic affairs, was the best solution for the difficulties which surrounded the Anglo-Irish relationship.

As a result of Isaac Butt's initiative the Home Rule Association was formed in Dublin in 1870 as a non-sectarian organisation, appealing to men of all political persuasions, and committed to the single aim of Home Rule for Ireland. In its early days the Association won little support from Irish Catholics, since most of them still pinned their faith on Gladstone and the Liberal Party, though a few members, including Butt who was returned for Limerick in 1871, were elected at by-elections as Home Rulers. But when the leaders of the Association widened their programme to include such popular issues as tenant right, they began to build up more support among the Irish electors. In 1873 the Association was replaced by a more distinctly political organisation, the Home Rule League. The moment was well chosen. For at the beginning of that year (as we saw in the previous section) Gladstone had incurred the wrath of the Roman Catholic Church and many Irish Liberal MPs over his Universities Bill, and it was in fact rejected by the House of Commons in March. This meant that the Irish electorate began to look with more sympathy on the claims of the Home Rule League.

The organisation of the League had hardly got off the ground before it was faced by a general election early in 1874. Nevertheless, the League won 59 seats: a verdict which reflected the astonishing decline of the Liberal Party in Ireland from 66 seats in 1868 to 12 seats now. This remarkable result was probably also helped by the 1872 Ballot Act which, by introducing the secret ballot at elections, undermined the electoral pressure normally exerted by the traditional parties. When parliament re-assembled in February 1874 after Disraeli's triumph at the polls, Isaac Butt and his followers constituted themselves into an independent Home Rule Party with their own officials and organisation.

The Home Rule Party, however, had little impact on the House of Commons or English public opinion generally. Part of the fault lay with the character of the party itself: apart from the general commitment to Home Rule, it lacked any real unity in ideas, organisation or membership. Moreover, even the commitment to Home Rule itself did little to bind the party together. For in reality only about a third of the members were genuine Home Rulers in the spirit of Butt: some were Fenians and many were really crypto-Liberals who had only jumped on the Home Rule bandwagon in 1874 in order to ensure their election as MPs.

All these faults were worsened by the weak leadership of Isaac Butt himself. He lacked the single-mindedness and ruthlessness, and the ability to inspire his followers, of the dedicated national leader. Often he was away from the House of Commons pursuing his legal career; and, even when present, his innate conservatism made him deferential to the established practices of parliament and conciliatory towards the traditional parties and their leaders. He was even sympathetic to Disraeli's imperial policies! Thus Butt was unable or unwilling to impose his own leadership and discipline upon the Home Rule Party in order to weld it into a powerful, cohesive instrument for forcing the House of Commons to consider seriously Irish claims.

Inevitably, Butt's leadership was soon challenged by a group of more militant Home Rulers. In 1875 J.C. Biggar and John O'Connor Power, both Fenians, began to apply the tactics of 'obstruction' in the House of Commons. This involved interminable speeches on Irish affairs, whatever subject was being debated at the time, in order to disrupt parliamentary business and focus the attention of the House on Irish grievances. Biggar and Power were soon joined by a more charismatic figure: Charles Stewart Parnell, a young Protestant landowner.

PROFILE: CHARLES STEWART PARNELL (1846–91)

-Profile-

Parnell was born in June 1846 into one of the greatest families of the Protestant Ascendancy, which had been established in County Wicklow since the later seventeenth century. Its members had held high office in the Irish government in the eighteenth century and had sat in the House of Commons after the Union. He was educated at schools in England and at the University of Cambridge, though he left without taking a degree. He then returned to Ireland and lived the life of a typical Anglo-Irish country squire. It was not until 1874 that he began to consider seriously a career in politics, partly out of a growing awareness of himself as an Irish nationalist. His mother was an important influence here, since she was American with a family tradition of anti-English feeling, and had been responsible for her son's upbringing since the early death of her husband when her son was only 13. Parnell's mother had some sympathy with the Fenians in the 1860s. But her son regarded their commitment to force as futile; and, though he was prepared to accept their support later, he remained convinced throughout his life that real change for Ireland could only come through the Westminster parliament.

Parnell was elected as a Home Ruler for the Irish constituency of Meath at a by-election in 1875, aged 29. He was tall, handsome, proud and reserved, and already possessed a commanding personality. In his early days he was a poor speaker – hesitant and highly strung. However, through sheer force of will and determination, he turned himself into an effective MP and a capable orator, particularly to mass audiences. As one of his followers later wrote: 'the strength of Parnell was character rather than intellect'. Within the House of Commons his support for obstruction meant that he identified himself with the militant section of the Home Rule Party which was critical of Butt's leadership. 'What did we ever get in the past by trying to conciliate?' he asked.

Later he established himself as the greatest Irish leader since O'Connell, the Protestant leader of a Catholic nation. He was known as 'the uncrowned King of Ireland' before disaster struck, with the O'Shea divorce (see page 88). He died in 1891, having failed to achieve Home Rule. Yet he had succeeded remarkably in his campaign for land reform, and, despite what his opponents and some supporters said, had pursued a constitutional path that rejected violence. He talked daggers, commented a colleague, but used none.

Parnell's aggressive attitude and contempt for English opinion soon made him a popular hero for militant Irish nationalists everywhere, and in 1877 he was elected President of the Home Rule Confederation of Great Britain. This was a bitter blow to the prestige of Isaac Butt, whose power was clearly waning. Parnell also had private contacts with a number of leading Fenians in 1877–8, and though he refused to commit himself to their revolutionary programme, they were impressed and prepared to co-operate. 'He has many of the qualities of leadership', wrote one Fenian leader to a colleague, 'and time will give him more'.

But Parnell made no attempt as yet to challenge directly Butt's position as leader of the Home Rule Party. However, the whole situation was completely transformed by the advent of agricultural depression in Ireland in 1879. The Irish national cause now became linked with the agrarian crisis.

3 Parnell and the Land League

> **KEY ISSUE** How did the activities of the Land League help Parnell's rise?

After the years of relative prosperity following the end of the Great Famine, Irish farmers found themselves faced with agricultural depression at the end of the 1870s. This was the result of a series of poor harvests in 1877–9, accompanied by the re-appearance of famine in the west of Ireland owing to the failure of the potato crop.

Another contributory factor, which affected England as well, was the import of cheap grain from America. All this was followed by a slump in food prices, including the prices of Irish cattle and dairy produce. The Irish smallholder also suffered from the drying up of oppor-tunities for migratory work in England owing to the impact of the depression there. The overall effect of the agricultural depression in Ireland was a drastic fall in farmers' incomes, and they responded by demanding the reduction or the remittance of rents. Though many landlords were prepared to accede initially, in the end non-payment by tenants led to evictions. In 1879 about 1,000 families (6,000 people) were turned off the land. Since the tenants had been demanding 'fair rents' for many years (a topic virtually untouched by the 1870 Land Act), and farmers' organisations existed in many parts of the country, all the material was now present for the creation of a popular agrarian movement directed against the landlords. What was needed was organisation and leadership on a national scale, and this was soon forthcoming. So too was violence, which never lay far below the surface in rural Ireland. Thus began the so-called 'Land War' of 1879–82.

The key figure in this was Michael Davitt. Davitt's family had been evicted from their smallholding in the west of Ireland in 1851 and emigrated to Lancashire, where as a boy young Davitt worked in the cotton mills. All this left him with a burning hatred of the landlord class in Ireland and of English domination. Later, he joined the Fenians and was arrested in 1870 for arms trafficking and served seven years in prison. On his release Davitt rejoined the Fenians – though unlike the hard-liners he now believed in co-operation with the constitutional nationalists. In 1878 he visited the United States. There he met the American Fenian John Devoy, whose views were similar to his own, and Devoy encouraged him to work for land reform and self-government in Ireland.

Back home Davitt was now determined to place the land question at the centre of Irish politics, for he believed that agrarian agitation by itself could force the government to yield to Irish demands for con-stitutional change as well as land reform. In the spring of 1879 he therefore threw himself into the smallholders' struggle in County Mayo (where he had been born) against the landlords, and began organising meetings and demonstrations in opposition to evictions and in favour of 'fair rents' and land reform. He also encouraged Parnell, whom he recognised as the up-and-coming leader of the rad-ical section of the Irish Parliamentary Party, to support the agitation. After some hesitation, Parnell agreed to speak at the great demon-stration at Westport in June 1879, where he appealed to the small-holders to 'hold a firm grip of your homesteads and lands'. More importantly perhaps, this was part of Parnell's calculated preparation for the leadership struggle within the Parliamentary Party, following

Butt's death in the previous month. Davitt later recorded his first impressions of Parnell.

> He struck me at once with the power and directness of his personality.
> There was the proud, resolute bearing of a man of conscious strength,
> with a mission, wearing no affectation, but without a hint of Celtic char-
> 5 acter or a trait of its racial enthusiasm. An Englishman of the strongest
> type, moulded for an Irish purpose ... [Later] I asked him to join the
> revolutionary organisation ... He then said slowly but clearly: 'No, I will
> never join any political secret society ... ' Mr Parnell never went in
> thought or in act a revolutionary inch, as an Irish nationalist, further
> than Henry Grattan.

In an attempt to use the land agitation as a battering ram for the Irish nationalist cause, Davitt followed up these early successes by arranging the famous meeting between himself, John Devoy and Parnell, at Dublin in June 1879. There the three men – symbolically representing agrarian radicalism, revolutionary nationalism and constitutional nationalism – came to an informal agreement in support of the tenants' demands and Irish self-government. This agreement marks the beginning of what is known in Irish history as the 'New Departure': 'it represents', in the words of one historian, 'the fusing into one national movement of all the elements of Irish protest and grievance'.

The tenants' movement now spread from the west to the more prosperous south and east and began to win support from the larger farmers. In October 1879 Davitt formed the Irish National Land League – with the watchword 'the Land for the People' – largely funded by Irish-American money; and Parnell agreed to become President. What were Parnell's motives in supporting the tenants' agitation? Though he did agree with their immediate demands for the '3 Fs' (Fixity of Tenure, Free Sale, Fair Rents), and, eventually, the buying out of the landlords, Parnell was never as radical a land reformer as Davitt (who supported, ultimately, land nationalisation), and he was more sympathetic to the Irish landlords – he was, after all, one himself! His motives were primarily political. Support for a popular agrarian movement would, he believed, encourage the cause of constitutional nationalism in Ireland and give leverage to the Home Rulers at Westminster, and thus help to wrest Home Rule from parliament. 'I would not have taken off my coat', he proclaimed, 'and gone to this work if I had not known that we were laying the foundation in this movement for the regeneration of our legislative independence'. He also argued that the agitation would force the British government to introduce land reform, and that this would help to bring to an end the conflict between tenants and landlords and encourage the latter to throw their weight behind the Home Rule movement. 'Deprive this [landlord] class of their privileges', he said at Liverpool in November 1879, 'show them that they must cast themselves in with the rest of their countrymen ... [and] the last knell of English power ... in Ireland has been sounded'.

It is this emphasis on the possibility of winning the landlord class for the nationalist cause that forms the most original part of Parnell's views on land reform, as Paul Bew has argued in his study of the Irish leader. This marks off Parnell from the outlook of Davitt and the Fenians, both of whom aimed at the elimination of, rather than co-operation with, the landlords. But Parnell was enough of a landed gentleman himself to hope that a self-governing Ireland would be ruled by men of position and influence – an outlook not dissimilar from Gladstone's later views. Furthermore, Parnell believed that support for the Irish tenantry would strengthen his own position against the moderates within the Irish Parliamentary Party. For, following the death of Isaac Butt in May 1879, another colourless moderate, William Shaw, had been elected temporary leader, but he proved incapable of uniting the party.

The aims of the Land League, as indicated in one of their posters, were:

1   First, to put an end to Rack-renting, Eviction, and Landlord Oppression.

Second, to effect such a radical change in the Land System of Ireland as will put it in the power of every Irish farmer to become the owner,
5 on fair terms, of the land he tills.

The means proposed to effect this object are:

(1) Organisation among the people and Tenant Farmers for the purpose of self-defence.

(2) The cultivation of public opinion by persistent exposure ... of the
10 monstrous injustice of the present system ...

(3) A resolute demand for the reduction of the excessive rents which have brought the Irish people to a state of starvation.

(4) Temperate but firm resistance to oppression and injustice.

This manifesto was of course largely propaganda. No reputable historian now regards the Land War as a simple clash between a rapacious landlord class and a down-trodden, exploited peasantry. Indeed it has been suggested by a number of recent historians that the real motive of the League's members in attacking the landlords and demanding the '3 Fs', was to enable them – and more particularly the larger pastoral farmers – to jack up their dwindling incomes by obtaining rent reductions (i.e., 'fair rents', in their eyes). The landlord was thus made the scapegoat for the effects of the agricultural depression.

Under the leadership of Davitt and his supporters the Land League became a weapon of popular protest against the landlord class, and, in day-to-day terms, concerned particularly with the problems of eviction. Between 1879 and 1883 some 14,600 tenants were turned off the land – more than in the previous 30 years. The League urged tenants to offer landlords lower rents or no rents, it helped tenants who were evicted and cared for the families of those who were imprisoned. It also applied a boycott against farmers who attempted to take over the holding of an evicted tenant. In Parnell's famous words in County Clare in September 1880, such a man should be dealt with, he urged, 'by putting him into a moral Coventry, by isolating him from the rest of his kind as if he was a leper of old'. Such tactics were also applied against the evicting landlords themselves, such as the famous Boycott whose name now became used to denote such practices.

Despite the public commitment of the tenants' leaders to peaceful protest, it was virtually certain that violence would erupt given the emotions aroused by eviction and the inflammatory language used in the Land League's propaganda. 'Outrages' against the landlords and their supporters became the characteristic feature of the Land War: 2,590 incidents were reported in 1880. This meant murders (there were 67 in the years 1879 to 1882), as well as assaults, intimidation, threatening letters, and attacks on property and animals. All this placed the authorities in an intolerable position in 1879–80. The Land League was a legal organisation and could not easily be prosecuted. Police and troops were used to protect persons and property; but the sporadic and varied nature of the outrages – generally perpetrated at night when 'Captain Moonlight' stalked the land – and the silent acquiescence of the local populace made the whole situation difficult to control.

Violence also raised problems for constitutionalists such as Parnell, since it was difficult to dissociate the outrages completely from the activities of the Land League of which he was President. Parnell, however, was away in America during the early months of 1880 raising money for the League and spreading the gospel of Irish nationalism. It was also an important move in his personal campaign for the leadership of the Irish Parliamentary Party. The American trip was an enormous success – financially and personally. Parnell addressed audiences in 62 cities and appealed deliberately and effectively to every section of Irish-American opinion.

Parnell cut short his American tour to return home and fight the general election of April 1880. That election led to an outstanding victory for the Liberals and the formation of Gladstone's Second Ministry. At the same time 61 Home Rulers were returned to parliament, including many new members sympathetic to Parnell. On 17 May 1880, at a meeting at the City Hall in Dublin, Parnell was elected leader of the Irish Parliamentary Party, receiving 23 votes to William Shaw's 18. The result showed that though his abilities were recognised, there was still much resentment against him by the moderates because of his association with agrarian radicalism and the Fenians. The problems of unity in the party therefore still remained. Nevertheless, after only five years in politics, and at the age of 34,

Charles Stewart Parnell had become leader of the Irish Parliamentary Party. The rise of Parnell, in the words of one historian, 'constitutes the most brilliant political performance in Irish history'.

4 Gladstone and Parnell, 1880–2

KEY ISSUE How was it that Gladstone and Parnell were able to reach substantial agreement by 1882?

a) The Second Land Act 1881

The general election of 1880 was not fought by Gladstone on Irish issues, but primarily on Disraeli's record in foreign and imperial affairs. Indeed, it was his outrage at the 'immorality' of Disraeli's Eastern policy (which involved diplomatic support for the Turks against their Christian rebels in the Balkans), which had led Gladstone to re-enter politics after his retirement from the Liberal leadership in 1875. Now, becoming Prime Minister for the second time, Gladstone had no plans for further Irish reform; in fact, apart from a vague commitment to franchise and local government reform, the Liberals came into power in 1880 with no definite programme at all.

Nevertheless, Ireland soon emerged as a major problem. As Gladstone admitted frankly in 1884: 'I did not know, no one knew, the severity of the crisis that was already swelling upon the horizon, and that shortly after rushed upon us like a flood'. What changed his attitude was his belief that Ireland now faced a social revolution as a result of the activities of the Land League and the outrages which seemed to accompany them. Violence increased substantially in the second half of 1880, exacerbated by the Lords' rejection of a Bill to protect from eviction tenants who were in arrears of rent. The only long-term solution to this crisis, Gladstone insisted, was further land reform.

The Prime Minister eventually accepted that exceptional powers of arrest and imprisonment must first be granted to the authorities, as W.E. Forster, the Irish Secretary, had been urging for some time. Early in 1881 the government therefore introduced a tough new Coercion Bill. This was opposed by the Irish Party led by Parnell for 41 hours (from 31 January to 2 February) using the by-now-familiar tactics of obstruction, until, on his own initiative, the Speaker brought the debate to an end by using the unprecedented device of the 'guillotine'. The Bill was soon passed. Since the Commons subsequently approved the new procedure, obstruction on the Irish model became almost impossible. Then on 3 February Michael Davitt was arrested and imprisoned under the new Act, an event that soon led to uproar in the House, followed by the suspension and expulsion of 36 Irish MPs including Parnell.

These events in fact played into the hands of the new Irish leader. For the vigour displayed by the Irish MPs in their opposition to the Coercion Bill, as well as the outrage aroused by the expulsions, helped to unify and strengthen the Irish Parliamentary Party and increased the personal prestige and authority its leader. This was emphasised by Parnell's deliberate refusal to support a 'No Rent' campaign, or to authorise the secession of the Irish Party from the House of Commons, in response to the militants' demands in protest at the government's repressive policies.

'Strangling the Monster' – *Punch*, 5 February, 1881

Coercion was followed a few months later by Gladstone's Second Land Act. Given the demands of the Land League and the recommendations of the government-appointed Bessborough Commission on the workings of the 1870 Land Act, the major terms of the new measure were almost pre-determined. In effect the Second Land Act of 1881 introduced the '3Fs'. (1) 'Fair Rents' for tenants, which were to be fixed for 15 years by Land Courts. (2) 'Fixity of Tenure' throughout Ireland, which meant that tenants could not be evicted providing they paid their rents. (3) 'Free Sale', which was the recog-. nition of the tenant's 'interest' in his holding and his right to compensation when he relinquished it. In addition, the government again included a land purchase scheme. This time it was rather more favourable to the tenant since it raised the state's proportion of the purchase price from two-thirds to three-quarters.

Despite his masterly performance in pushing the complicated Land Bill through the Commons in the summer of 1881 (followed by the acquiescence of the Lords), recent historians have argued that Gladstone again failed to face up to the economic realities of rural Ireland. For in the west of Ireland particularly, it was the lack of cultivable land rather than the problem of rents that was the fundamental problem for the smallholders – hence the emphasis on land reclamation and improvement by some land reformers. But the Second Land Act has been described as 'less an economic policy than ... a political stroke'. For Gladstone its purpose was to destroy the *raison d'être* of the Land League and the necessity for violence by granting the tenants their major demands. To a large extent he succeeded – thanks to the work of the Land Courts. For, owing to their decisions, over the next few years a 20 per cent reduction in rents gradually occurred. This harsh economic fact, together with their rapidly declining morale as a result of their general unpopularity, did lead the landlord class in Ireland seriously to consider selling-off their estates, though the land purchase clauses of the recent Act were still regarded as insufficiently generous by most tenants to induce them to consider buying their holdings.

b) The Kilmainham Treaty 1882

The passage of the Second Land Act also faced Parnell with a real dilemma. As Irish leader he had to maintain the support of both the militants and the moderates inside his own party and within the wider Irish communities in the United Kingdom and America. If he supported the Land Act he would be denounced by the militants for currying favour with the Liberals and abandoning the struggle for fundamental land reform; if he opposed it, he might lose the support of the moderates and antagonise those tenants who saw tangible benefits in the Act. Parnell therefore played for time: he criticised aspects of the Act (such as the exclusion of tenants in arrears from its provisions) without absolutely rejecting it, but refused to co-operate with the working of the Land Courts. However, Parnell was soon rescued from his dilemma by the obtuseness of the government.

In October 1881 Gladstone warned the leaders of the Land League (with Parnell clearly in mind) in a public speech: 'If . . . there is to be fought a final conflict in Ireland between law on the one side and sheer lawlessness on the other . . . then I say . . . the resources of civilisation are not yet exhausted'. Parnell replied by denouncing the Liberal leader as 'a masquerading knight errant, the pretending champion of the rights of every other nation except those of the Irish nation'. Shortly afterwards, on the grounds that Parnell was deliberately wrecking the working of the Land Act, Forster had him arrested and imprisoned in Kilmainham Gaol in Dublin. It was (as the historian George Boyce comments) 'the best thing that could have happened to him'. It switched attention from Parnell's indecisiveness to the perfidy of Gladstone and Forster, and for all nationalist Irishmen it turned Parnell into a martyr for the cause. It also gave him time to reflect on the changing character of 'the Irish question', especially as his own imprisonment was soon followed by the banning of the Land League. 'Politically', he wrote to his mistress, Mrs Katharine O'Shea, 'it is a fortunate thing for me that I have been arrested, as the [national] movement is breaking fast and all will be quiet in a few months when I shall be released'.

Paradoxically, Parnell's arrest was the prelude to better relations between the Irish leader and the British government. Gladstone realised that the imprisonment of Parnell solved nothing: violence inevitably worsened rather than improved during his six-month incarceration. Only the 'uncrowned King of Ireland', it appeared, could control the level of law and order in his domain. Parnell on his side accepted that the situation in Ireland had now changed dramatically. The Land Act had defeated the Land League. Significantly, the tenants had earlier ignored the League's call for a 'No Rents' campaign, and were now busily using the new Land Courts to get their rents reduced legally. The Land War was effectively grinding to a halt. In these circumstances might it not be better for the cause of Irish nationalism to recognise facts and come to terms with the dominant Liberal Party? For Parnell this would also mean that he could re-assert his essential role as the leader of a constitutional Irish Party, committed to obtaining Home Rule through the parliamentary process. By the early months of 1882 Parnell also had personal reasons for wishing to be released from prison, since Kitty O'Shea was pregnant with his child and he wished to be with her.

Thus all the conditions were present for an agreement between Gladstone and Parnell. With Joseph Chamberlain, the outstanding Radical in the government, and Captain O'Shea (Katharine's husband!) acting as intermediaries, what became known as the 'Kilmainham Treaty' was rapidly concluded in April 1882. By its terms the government agreed to release Parnell and relax the Coercion Act, and also amend the Land Act so as to help those in arrears with their rent. In turn, Parnell agreed to use his influence against violence and to accept and support the carrying out of the recent Land Act, and especially the work of the Land Courts. He also agreed if the government carried out its side of the bargain 'to co-operate cordially for the future with the Liberal party in forwarding Liberal principles and measures of general reform'. W.E. Forster's response to the Kilmainham Treaty, concluded without his knowledge or agreement, was to resign.

The new accord between Gladstone and Parnell was shaken but not irretrievably damaged by the brutal murder of Lord Frederick Cavendish (Forster's successor as Irish Secretary) and T.H. Burke, the Under-Secretary, in Phoenix Park, Dublin, on 6 May, by an Irish revolutionary group known as 'The Invincibles'. The sincere shock and horror displayed by Parnell in response to the murders created a good impression in the House of Commons, and he was persuaded by Gladstone to abandon his original intention of giving up politics. The Phoenix Park murders were followed by a general reaction against political violence in the United Kingdom and the United States, though the new Irish Secretary (G.O. Trevelyan) felt compelled to impose new security measures. The events of 1882 thus drove home to Parnell and all political observers the basic fact now about the Irish situation: politics had superseded the agrarian struggle. Once again the fate of Ireland was centred on the House of Commons. As George Boyce comments: 'For better or for worse, for richer or poorer, the Home Rule Party was synonymous with nationalist Ireland.'

Summary Diagram

Gladstone and Irish Reform, 1868–82

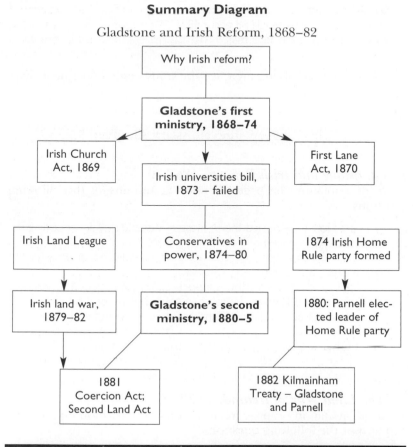

Why Irish reform?

Gladstone's first ministry, 1868–74

Irish Church Act, 1869

Irish universities bill, 1873 – failed

First Lane Act, 1870

Irish Land League

Conservatives in power, 1874–80

1874 Irish Home Rule party formed

Irish land war, 1879–82

Gladstone's second ministry, 1880–5

1880: Parnell elected leader of Home Rule party

1881 Coercion Act; Second Land Act

1882 Kilmainham Treaty – Gladstone and Parnell

Working on Chapter 5

Detailed notes are required on the Irish reforms of Gladstone's First and Second Ministries. A chronological approach is probably best. Try to show the interaction between events and policies. In conclusion, jot down notes on how successful Gladstone's Irish policies had been by 1882. This will provide a starting point for the next chapter, on Home Rule.

Answering structured and essay questions on Chapter 5

Structured question are basically factual. Consider, for instance, the following:

I   a)   Describe the policies Gladstone adopted towards Ireland in his first and second ministries.

b)   What were the most important developments in Irish nationalism that occurred between 1858 and 1882?
c)   What were Parnell's major characteristics as an Irish leader up to 1882?

For essay questions on this area, see the study guide to the next chapter.

Source-based questions on Chapter 5

1   Gladstone and Irish Reform, 1868–9
Read the quotations on pages 70 and 72, and answer the following questions.

a)   Why did Gladstone regard the Protestant Ascendancy as 'poisoning the atmosphere of the land of Ireland'? (*4 marks*)
b)   Comment on the style and character of Gladstone's oratory in this extract from his 1868 speech. (*5 marks*)
c)   Why did Gladstone gain the support of the Presbyterians, nonconformists and Irish Roman Catholics in the 1868 general election? Why were the Anglican clergy in England opposed to him then? (*7 marks*)
d)   What evidence can you point to in this chapter that shows the importance of the religious issue in the 1868 election? (*4 marks*)
e)   Why did the Irish Roman Catholics' hearts 'leap for joy' at the terms of Gladstone's Irish Church Act, 1869? (*5 marks*)

2   The Land War in Ireland, 1879–82
Read the quotation on page 82 and look at the cartoon on page 85, and answer the following questions.

a)   What particular examples of 'Landlord Oppression' did the Land League oppose? (*6 marks*)
b)   Explain briefly one example of 'self-defence' used by Irish tenants against the landlords. (*3 marks*)
c)   How fair is the League's view of the Irish landlords contained in statement (3)? (*6 marks*)
d)   Comment briefly on the portrayal of Gladstone and the supporters of the Land League contained in the cartoon. (*6 marks*)
e)   What were the 'remedial measures' illustrated here, passed by Gladstone in 1881? (*4 marks*)
f)   How important was the issue of land reform around this time? (*10 marks*)

6 Gladstone, Parnell and Home Rule

POINTS TO CONSIDER

Two Home Rule Bills were introduced, in 1886 and 1893, both of which failed to secure acceptance by parliament. You need to understand the reasons both for their introduction and their failure. This will involve examining the policies and motives of Gladstone, as well as appreciating the realities of political power in Britain during this period. The other key figure is Parnell, whose importance as a parliamentarian and nationalist you have to assess.

KEY DATES

1882   (October) formation of the National League
1885   (June) Parnell supported Conservatives, Gladstone resigned; Conservatives in power under Lord Salisbury; (November) general election: Irish Party won 86 seats and held the balance of power in the Commons; (December) Herbert Gladstone flew the 'Hawarden kite'
1886   (January) Parnell switched Irish votes to Liberals: Gladstone formed his Third Ministry; (April) Gladstone introduced First Home Rule Bill, which was defeated in the Commons
1887   (April) Parnell accused of complicity with terrorism
1889   (December) Captain O'Shea sued for divorce, citing Parnell as co-respondent
1890   (November) divorce granted; Gladstone opposed Parnell as Irish leader; (December) Irish Party split over leadership
1891   (October) death of Parnell
1892   (July) general election: Gladstone formed Fourth Ministry, with Irish support
1893   (September) Second Irish Home Rule Bill passed by Commons but rejected by Lords

1 Parnell and the Irish Parliamentary Party, 1882–5

> **KEY ISSUE** Why was Parnell in such a strong parliamentary position in this period?

After the Kilmainham Treaty (see page 87) Parnell was determined to turn the Home Rule group in the House of Commons into a powerful, unified Irish Party, subject completely to his own personal authority, a party which could really make its weight felt in British politics. At the same time he intended to make the Irish Parliamentary Party the dominant nationalist organisation in Ireland. The latter aim was forwarded by the creation of the National League in October 1882. Unlike the Land League (which had not survived its banning by the British authorities) the National League was essentially a political organisation; its first aim was 'national self-government', and it intended to win support among all classes of Irish society and not just the farmers. The National League's central organisation was dominated by Parnell and his followers, and the League became in effect the electoral arm of the Irish Parliamentary Party. It soon possessed over 1,000 branches throughout Ireland. The League's electoral role was helped enormously by the passage of the Third Reform Act of 1884. By granting the vote to the rural householders within the United Kingdom, the Act enabled the Parnellites to dominate the county vote throughout Ireland outside Protestant Ulster. This increasing identification between the Irish Parliamentary Party and the cause of Irish nationalism, was reflected – after years of mutual suspicion – by the unofficial alliance which was concluded between the Irish Catholic Church leaders and Parnell in 1885–6. The Church now came out definitely in support of Home Rule, and in return Parnell was prepared to go along with the Church's policies on education, though relations between the two sides were never very close.

As far as the Irish Party at Westminster was concerned, Parnell now imposed greater discipline and centralisation, a task which was made somewhat easier by the increasingly homogeneous, middle-class character of the party's membership, compared with the days of Isaac Butt. Parliamentary candidates were now chosen in practice by the party's leadership, and, if elected, they were required to sign a 'pledge' that they would act and vote only with the Irish Parliamentary Party. If they failed to do so, they would resign.

By the mid-1880s, therefore, Parnell completely dominated the Irish Party. Acknowledged by all members as 'the Chief', his power was, as one of his protégés later admitted, 'irresponsible and more or less despotic'. Parnell's personal traits of pride, coldness and arrogance had hardened over the years, and he was now viewed by his followers with a mixture of awe, respect and something akin almost to fear. His attitude towards them was (in the words of his biographer, Paul Bew) 'comparable to that of a feudal magnate towards his band of retainers: a curious blend of hauteur, autocracy and condescension'.

Yet whatever the Chief's personal faults, by 1885 his efforts on behalf of the Irish Parliamentary Party and the national cause generally seemed to have been extraordinarily successful. Now he really was 'the uncrowned King of Ireland', and was also acknowledged by everyone as an outstanding parliamentary leader. He was courted by both Liberals and Conservatives, since both groups recognised that his

Irish Party might well hold the balance of power in the Commons after the next general election, due in 1885.

The first move was made by Joseph Chamberlain, who was anxious to ensure not only a Liberal government after the election but the strengthening of his own personal position within the Liberal leadership. In order to obtain Parnell's support, he proposed to him a 'Central Board' scheme for Ireland which would have given the Irish wide-ranging powers of internal control: in Chamberlain's words, 'the widest possible self-government . . . consistent with the integrity of the Empire'. For Chamberlain (who was fundamentally an Imperialist) this was conceived as an alternative to Home Rule; but on those terms it had no possible chance of being accepted by Parnell. The scheme was in any case rejected by the Cabinet, despite Gladstone's support. In January 1885, in one of his most famous speeches in Ireland, Parnell reiterated his commitment to Home Rule – and perhaps more:

1   I do not know how this great question will eventually be settled. I do
    not know whether England will be wise in time, and concede to consti-
    tutional arguments and methods the restitution of that which was
    stolen from us towards the close of the last century . . . We cannot ask
5   for less than the restitution of Grattan's Parliament . . . But no man has
    a right to fix the boundary to the march of a nation. No man has a right
    to say to his country, 'thus far shalt thou go and no farther'.

Parnell now drew nearer to the Tories, hoping to get more from a Conservative government than from the Liberals. Nor was Parnell in principle opposed to a Conservative settlement of Ireland. As the Radical Henry Labouchere said with much truth, 'Home Rule apart, he was himself a Tory'. On 9 June 1885, therefore, the Irish Party switched their votes from Liberals to Conservatives; and as a result of numerous Liberal abstentions – a reflection of growing divisions within the party – Gladstone was out-voted and resigned. Lord Salisbury then formed a Conservative caretaker government until the results of the forthcoming general election were known.

The new government showed its good intentions by dropping coercion, and passing the Ashbourne Act – the first really effective land purchase scheme for Ireland, since it provided for 100 per cent state loans to tenants at a low rate of interest. For the moment, therefore, Parnell stood by the Tories, and, since Gladstone refused to commit himself publicly over Home Rule, in the general election in November 1885 he called upon the Irish voters in Great Britain to vote Conservative. Parnell demanded Home Rule – with powers as wide as possible for an Irish parliament – but insisted that it did not mean a complete separation from Great Britain.

In the election the Irish Parliamentary Party won every seat in Ireland south of eastern Ulster (with the exception of Trinity College, Dublin), and ended up with 86 seats. The Liberals won 335 seats and the Conservatives 249. The real victor in the election was Parnell, who had utterly destroyed the power of the Liberal Party in Ireland. More importantly, neither the Tories nor the Liberals could govern without his support, since his '86 of 86' (in the triumphant Irish phrase) equalled exactly the difference in numbers between the two English parties. Which of them he now decided to back would depend on the attitude of Salisbury and Gladstone towards Home Rule. The political situation was therefore highly confused when parliament reassembled in December 1885.

2 The First Home Rule Bill, 1886

> **KEY ISSUES** Why did Gladstone take up the cause of Home Rule? Why was the first Home Rule Bill lost?

Neither during the election campaign itself nor in its immediate aftermath would Gladstone commit himself publicly over Home Rule. Nevertheless, during the summer months of 1885, while brooding at home at Hawarden Castle on the realities of the Irish problem, he appears to have become convinced that Home Rule was the only solution. He now believed, despite his earlier optimism, that his programme of religious and agrarian reform had failed to reconcile the Irish to the continuance of English rule; and further reform was bound to be just as unsuccessful. Moreover, he became convinced of the reality of Irish nationalism, 'a collective or corporate individuality tested by reason and sufficiently confirmed by history'. How then on moral grounds could he oppose what a majority of the Irish people wanted? Indeed Gladstone came to believe that he had been singled out by Providence to lead a great moral crusade on behalf of the Irish people which would culminate in Home Rule and the solution of the Irish problem. Home Rule, he said, was based on 'the first principles of religion'.

During the run-up to the election in November 1885, however, Gladstone kept quiet about his conversion to Home Rule. Why was this? He seems to have been moved by several considerations. In the first place, if he spoke out publicly in favour of Home Rule, the break-up of the Liberal Party would inevitably follow. In addition (a charge to which he was particularly sensitive) he could be accused of counter-bidding for the Irish vote. Also, as J.L. Hammond argued in his sympathetic study of Gladstone's Irish policy, the Liberal leader believed, sincerely if naively, in achieving a non-party approach to the Irish problem. The Conservatives had come into power in June 1885 as a result of Parnell's conviction that he could get more from them than from the Liberals, and Gladstone realised the enormous advantages of a Home Rule policy introduced by Lord Salisbury, with his mastery of the House of Lords, backed up by the majority of Liberals. 'Every step he took between June 1885 and January 1886,' wrote Hammond, 'was a deliberate effort to obtain a solution by passionless co-operation among the leading statesmen'. It was these considerations that led Gladstone to keep silence, even to Parnell and his colleagues, during the election campaign at the end of 1885 and to acquiesce in Irish support for the Conservative party.

The outcome of the election was a disappointment for Gladstone in so far as it failed to provide either of the English parties with a real majority independent of the Irish members. On the other hand, the fact that the Irish Party won every seat in southern Ireland (bar one) clinched his support for Home Rule.

'I consider that Ireland has now spoken', he wrote to Lord Hartington on 17 December, 'and that an effort ought to be made by the government without delay to meet her demands for the management by an Irish legislative body of Irish as distinct from imperial affairs. Only a government can do it, and a tory government can do it more easily and safely than any other'.

Gladstone's hope, however, was utterly destroyed by the publication in the press on the very same day of the news of his support for Home Rule, as a result of the deliberate action of his son. Herbert Gladstone believed that Chamberlain and his Radical friends were planning to take over the Liberal Party, and the only way to forestall them was by encouraging Parnell to join with the Liberals and oust the Conservatives, and thus force his father to re-enter the political arena. Herbert Gladstone's action in 'flying the Hawarden kite' (as it was dubbed) was successful. Since it soon became clear that Lord Salisbury had no intention of supporting Home Rule, on 26 January 1886 the Irish deliberately supported a Liberal resolution on land reform, and the Conservatives were defeated by 331 votes to 252, though 76 Liberals abstained, and a few, led by Lord Hartington, actually voted with the government. The Liberal Party was clearly disintegrating. Nevertheless Gladstone now became Prime Minister for the third time, at the age of 77, committed to the introduction of Home Rule.

These events led John Vincent and A.B. Cooke in their major study of English parliamentary politics in 1885–6, *The Governing Passion* (1974), to argue that, for Gladstone, 'Ireland was viewed in a context of deep party calculation'. They suggest that Gladstone's support for Home Rule was due to opportunism rather than conviction: it was primarily an attempt to re-unite the Liberal Party under his own leadership and thus put paid to the ambitions of Joseph Chamberlain. 'The [Home Rule Bill]', they wrote, 'was meant to unite the Liberal Party by committing it to the principle of home rule and to prepare it for further protracted struggle in which there would be only one possible leader'. The whole argument is abstruse and controversial, and now seems difficult to sustain. For though we can accept that Gladstone was inevitably concerned with the future of the Liberal Party in 1885–6, there is abundant evidence that he was committed to Home Rule before the general election of November 1885; and, more recently, a number of historians have argued powerfully that it is impossible to understand Gladstone's politics without constant reference to his moral and religious outlook.

Following his accession to power in January 1886, Gladstone, determined 'to grasp the Irish nettle', proceeded with a Home Rule Bill swiftly and boldly. Earlier he had hoped to have time to educate the electorate and his party; now he believed (incorrectly as it turned out) that the potentially revolutionary situation developing in Ireland brooked no delay. In that sense he was (in Lord Randolph Churchill's famous comment) 'an old man in a hurry'. The task was undertaken in the worst possible circumstances since nearly all his colleagues (as well as Parnell) had been left completely in the dark about his change of attitude. Hartington and most of the Whig notables refused to join the government; other Liberals, such as Chamberlain and Trevelyan, did so reluctantly but later resigned when the details of the Home Rule Bill became known.

The Home Rule package was presented to the Cabinet in March 1886, and consisted of two closely related Bills which aimed to solve the political and the social problems of Ireland together. The first Bill proposed the establishment of a bi-cameral Irish legislature, consisting of two Orders which would sit and vote together. The first Order – a sort of Upper House – was weighted in favour of property and was to contain a number of Irish peers; the second Order consisted entirely of MPs elected in the ordinary way. From the legislature would be drawn the Irish executive, which was to be responsible to it, though the Lord-Lieutenant would still remain as the Queen's representative. The Irish legislature would have the right to deal with all Irish affairs, except those enumerated as belonging to the Imperial government at Westminster: the most important of these were defence, foreign policy, international trade, customs and excise and (temporarily) the Irish police. It was proposed that Ireland contribute one-fifteenth to the Imperial Treasury, but would of course receive back her share of customs revenue and income tax. Irish MPs were to be excluded from Westminster. This avoided the complicated problem of deciding what debates they should be allowed to attend if they remained members of the House of Commons. But for Gladstone exclusion was necessary principally in order to ensure that the proposed Irish parliament began its life with the undivided loyalty of its members and thus gained respect and authority.

The second Bill consisted of a land purchase scheme by which the British Treasury would buy out the landlords at a cost of some £50 million. Gladstone believed this was essential in order to prevent the new Irish legislature being burdened at the outset with the problems of the Irish land system. He also hoped that this would lead eventually to the former landlord class re-asserting their influence in the social and political affairs of Ireland – a view with which Parnell was sympathetic.

The Prime Minister presented his Home Rule Bill to the House of Commons on 8 April 1886 in a great three-and-a-half hour speech. The Land Purchase Bill was soon abandoned when it became apparent that it was unpopular with all sections of opinion in the House, though Gladstone hoped to re-introduce it later. The debates which followed centred therefore on the provisions concerning the government of Ireland. Gladstone elaborated in greater detail the main reasons which had already led him to adopt Home Rule, and the solutions he proposed. He touched briefly on the problem of Ulster, which he did not take very seriously. He ended his speech with his famous appeal to the House of Commons, for he believed that his bill represented probably the last chance for solving the Irish question peacefully:

1 While I think it is right to modify the Union in some particulars, we are not about to propose its repeal ... That authority of the Imperial Parliament ... as established by the Act of Union ... it is not asked ... and certainly it is not intended in the slightest degree to impair ... The
5 fault of the administrative system of Ireland ... is simply this – that its spring and source of action ... is English and not Irish ... what we seek is the settlement of that question; and we think we find that settlement in the establishment ... of a legislative body sitting in Dublin for the conduct of both legislation and administration under the conditions ...
10 defining Irish as distinct from Imperial affairs ... I cannot conceal the conviction that the voice of Ireland, as a whole, has at this moment clearly and constitutionally spoken ... when five-sixths of its lawfully chosen representatives are of one mind in this matter ... I cannot allow it to be said that a Protestant minority in Ulster or elsewhere is to rule
15 the question at large for Ireland ... We stand face to face with what is termed Irish nationality [which] vents itself in the demand for local autonomy ... Is that an evil in itself? ... I hold that it is not ... The Irishman is profoundly Irish, but it does not follow that because his local patriotism is keen he is incapable of Imperial patriotism ... Think, I
20 beseech you; think well, think wisely, think not for the moment, but for the years that are to come before you reject this bill.

The bulk of the members of the Parliamentary Liberal Party supported Gladstone. This was not because they accepted his arguments over Irish nationality or had much enthusiasm for Irish self-government, but out of loyalty to the 'Grand Old Man' and because they could see no alternative to Home Rule but perpetual coercion – and they no longer had any stomach for that. Parnell had doubts about some of the details, particularly the financial provisions, which he believed were unfair to Ireland; but he supported the Home Rule Bill. 'I accept the Bill', he pronounced in the House of Commons, 'as a

A Cartoon from the *Illustrated London News*, 24 April, 1886

final settlement of our national question and I believe the Irish people will accept it'. But the Bill was bitterly attacked by the Conservatives, and by many leading Liberals, such as Lord Hartington and Joseph Chamberlain. Though there was some crude anti-Irish feeling displayed in the debates, many of the points they made against the Bill were reasoned and cogent. Three major criticisms were directed against Gladstone's proposals. First, it was argued that Irish self-government would lead inevitably to complete separation and therefore the break-up of the United Kingdom, especially as Ireland was not to be represented at Westminster. Secondly, critics questioned whether the members of the future Irish legislature could be trusted to protect even-handedly the lives and property of all Irishmen, and especially Protestants, when many of those MPs would inevitably be nationalists who had been associated with illegality and agitation in the past. Thirdly, it was argued that Irish nationality and unity (the rock on which Gladstone appeared to rest his case) could not really be said to exist when all classes in Protestant Ulster were so violently against Home Rule.

Towards the end of the debates, on 27 May, Gladstone called a meeting of his supporters in the Parliamentary Liberal Party to discuss the position: Hartington and Chamberlain obviously did not attend, though some of the latter's supporters did. The only concession Gladstone was prepared to make was to reconsider the exclusion of the Irish MPs from Westminster; but his whole tone was angry and autocratic and he made no real effort to win over the waverers. Four days later Chamberlain called a meeting of the Liberal anti-Home Rulers: 55 MPs turned up: with the support of the veteran Radical John Bright, they decided to vote against the Bill. Thus, on 8 June 1886, when the vote was finally taken on the Second Reading of the Home Rule Bill, 93 Liberals were against, and it was defeated by 313 votes to 343.

Parliament was then dissolved and the parties squared up for the second general election within a year. The Conservatives, united and confident, fought a vigorous campaign and relied heavily on the anti-Irish sentiments of the majority of the English voters. They also worked effectively to produce a Unionist victory by making sure that Liberal Unionists (as the Liberal anti-Home Rulers were now called) were unopposed by Tory candidates. The Liberal Party, which was now split down the middle and had lost its most able leaders apart from Gladstone, was in a desperately weak position. During the election campaign it relied mainly on Gladstone's prestige. This still had potency in the 'Celtic fringe' (Wales and Scotland) where the Liberals did reasonably well; and the Irish, though they fought as a separate party under Parnell, were inevitably tied to the Liberals as the only English party now committed to Home Rule. Yet the outcome of the election in the summer of 1886 was a resounding victory for the Unionists. They won 394 seats (316 Conservatives, 78 Liberal

Unionists); the Gladstonian Liberals were reduced to 191 MPs, backed up by the Irish Party of 85 members. Clearly for the moment Home Rule was a lost cause: Ireland was to face nearly 20 years of 'resolute government' (in Lord Salisbury's phrase) under the Unionists.

3 The Fall of Parnell

> **KEY ISSUES** What led to Parnell's political eclipse? What achievements stand to his credit?

After the general election of 1886 the Irish Parliamentary Party still dominated the representation of Ireland outside Protestant Ulster, and Parnell remained determined to stick to the constitutional path in securing Home Rule. This meant, he believed, maintaining the alliance with the Liberal Party which, under its aged and obstinate leader, was still committed to the same ideal. Parnell therefore refused to support the new phase of agrarian agitation in Ireland known as the 'Plan of Campaign', which aimed at reducing rents still further by collective action by the tenants, since this might endanger the alliance. Both the Liberals and the Irish were at one, however, in condemning the harsh, coercive measures introduced by the new Conservative Irish Secretary, A.J. Balfour, in 1887, in order to break the power of the Campaign.

   That same year *The Times* published a vindictive series of articles, 'Parnellism and Crime', which accused the Irish leader of complicity in violence in Ireland, and, in particular, of approval of the Phoenix Park Murders. In 1889, however, a judicial investigation revealed that the articles were based on forged letters. The editor of *The Times*, who had paid £2,500 for the letters, had believed them genuine because he wanted them to be. The forger blew his brains out in a Madrid hotel. The ignominious collapse of the case against Parnell led to a wave of public sympathy for the Irishman. In December 1889 Gladstone, in a pointed gesture, invited him to visit Hawarden Castle. Yet within a year Parnell's personal reputation and his political career were virtually in ruins.

   This was the result of the notorious divorce case in which he was now involved. For in the very month of his Hawarden visit, Captain O'Shea filed suit for divorce, citing Parnell as co-respondent on the grounds of his adultery with Mrs Katharine O'Shea. The case came to court in November 1890: Parnell offered no defence and O'Shea was granted his divorce. At first, the divorce seemed to have no political repercussions, and the Irish Parliamentary Party stood by its leader. But Gladstone soon found himself under pressure from the powerful nonconformist element in the Liberal Party, who refused to accept alliance with a party whose leader was a confessed adulterer.

Gladstone felt he therefore had no alternative but to urge the Irish to repudiate Parnell as their leader if the alliance – and therefore the cause of Home Rule – was to be maintained. In a letter to Justin MacCarthy (Parnell's second-in-command) he spelt out the position:

1   The conclusion at which ... I had myself arrived ... was that notwith-
standing the splendid services rendered by Mr Parnell to his country, his
continuance at the present moment in the leadership would be productive of consequences disastrous in the highest degree to the cause
5   of Ireland ... the continuance I speak of would not only place many
hearty and effective friends of the Irish cause in a position of great
embarrassment, but would render my retention of the leadership of the
liberal party, based as it has been mainly upon the prosecution of the
Irish cause, almost a nullity.

When this letter was eventually published in the press at the end of November, Parnell reacted furiously. He not only refused to resign the leadership – even temporarily – but in an extraordinary manifesto to the Irish people attacked Gladstone personally, denounced the Liberal alliance and re-affirmed the independence of the Irish Party. Thus he appeared to throw overboard the whole political strategy he had cultivated so assiduously over the previous five years. Irish Nationalist MPs were therefore faced with a cruel dilemma: if they stood by Parnell they would lose Liberal support and, apparently, any further possibility of Home Rule. They had to choose, as one con-temporary put it, 'between Parnell and Parnellite principles'. At the historic meeting of the Irish Parliamentary Party at the House of Commons on 1 December 1890, the party split: 45 MPs (led by MacCarthy) repudiated Parnell's leadership, 37 supported him. As Timothy Healy, one of Parnell's bitterest opponents, insisted: 'I say that the necessities of Ireland are paramount'. A few days later – another nail in Parnell's coffin – the leaders of the Irish Catholic clergy called upon the Irish people to repudiate him.

Parnell reacted to all his enemies with characteristic defiance. In the summer of 1891 he fought one last campaign in Ireland at a series of by-elections. Here he even appeared to countenance the abandon-ment of constitutional methods in the pursuit of Irish freedom. In all these by-elections, however, the anti-Parnellites triumphed. Parnell was now ill and worn-out, and he died on 6 October 1891 at Brighton in the arms of his wife Kitty (as the former Mrs O'Shea had now become). He was only 45.

Years later his old colleague, Michael Davitt, attempted to sum up his character:

1   Parnell's claim to greatness no Irish nationalist and few Irishmen will
ever deny ... Like all the world's historic characters, there were
marked limitations to his greatness, not counting the final weakness
which precipitated his fall ... He was unlike all the leaders who had
5   preceded him in his accomplishments, traits of character and personal

idiosyncrasies ... In fact he was a paradox in Irish leadership ... bearing
no resemblance of any kind to those who handed down to his time the
fight for Irish nationhood ... What, then, was the secret of his immense
influence and popularity? He was above and before everything else a
10 splendid fighter. He had attacked and beaten the enemies of Ireland in
the citadel of their power – the British Parliament.

Charles Stewart Parnell was a controversial figure in his lifetime, and
he has remained so ever since. Yet most historians are now agreed on
the nature of his contribution to Anglo-Irish history. For though
Parnell was associated with the Land League, and, at the height of his
power, was regarded as the embodiment of Irish nationalism, he was
pre-eminently a practical politician rather than an agrarian reformer
or an agitator or a romantic nationalist. In the political field his
achievement was two-fold. In the first place, he turned the question of
Home Rule from a vague ideal into practical politics. He 'set it on its
legs', as Gladstone said, by his belief that it must be worked for and
could be achieved constitutionally through the British parliament by
the exercise of political skill and judgement, even though (like
Gladstone) he underestimated the enormous problems that surrounded the whole conception. In particular, he had no understanding of, or sympathy with, the aspirations of the Ulster Protestants.
Even more remarkably, Parnell was eventually able to convince the
majority of the Irish people that Home Rule was both a just and a feas-
ible solution to the problem of Irish government. Moreover, it was his
consistent and convincing support for Home Rule – as shown in the
triumph of his party in Ireland in the general election of November
1885 – that helped to clinch Gladstone's conversion to that cause
during the previous summer. Thereafter, by throwing the weight of
the Irish Parliamentary Party on to the Liberal side in January 1886,
Parnell made the passage of Gladstone's First Home Rule Bill in the
Commons a realistic possibility, even though in the end the unexpected revolt of so many Liberals confounded them both.

This points to Parnell's second great political achievement: his creation of a united, disciplined Irish Parliamentary Party backed up by
an efficient electoral machine in Ireland itself. Not that Parnell was by
any means an ideal party leader. His touchiness, his aloofness, his evident contempt for many of his colleagues, and his frequent absences
from parliamentary business to stay with Kitty O'Shea – all probably
help to account for the reaction against him at the fateful party meeting on 1 December 1890, even apart from Gladstone's ultimatum conveyed in his letter to Justin MacCarthy. Nevertheless, the Irish Party
under Parnell's leadership played a key role in British politics and in
the history of the Irish question during the 1880s, largely as a result
of his political realism and sensitivity to the workings of the British
party system. It is true that after Parnell's death in 1891 the Irish
Parliamentary Party – divided and leaderless – was only a shadow of its

former self, a decline which was exacerbated by the defeat of the Second Home Rule Bill in 1893 and the subsequent domination of the Unionists. Nevertheless, the Irish Parliamentary Party survived, and, re-united under the Parnellite John Redmond, in 1900, it re-emerged as an important factor in British politics during the Liberal ascendancy after 1906 (developments discussed in the next chapter.)

4 The Second Home Rule Bill, 1893

KEY ISSUES Why did the Second Home Rule Bill fail? Were Gladstone's efforts realistic?

Despite grumblings from many party members anxious to free themselves from the Irish burden and turn their attention to social and economic reform, Gladstone remained firmly committed to Home Rule as his major objective. The Liberal Party therefore felt it had no alternative but to follow where he led. In the 1892 general election the Liberals made a considerable recovery (owing mainly to working-class discontent with Tory social and economic policies) and gained about 80 seats. With 273 MPs the Liberals were still in a minority compared to the Conservatives (with 269 MPs and the support of 46 Liberal Unionists); but 80 Irish Nationalists were elected, the majority of whom were anti-Parnellites, and with their support Gladstone (now aged 84) was able to form his Fourth Ministry.

Gladstone discussed a proposed new Home Rule Bill with his colleagues and both Parnellite and anti-Parnellite Irish MPs. As a result it differed in several ways from the earlier bill. The financial provisions were made more favourable to the Irish; and it was also agreed that 80 Irish MPs should be retained at Westminster, where they were to be allowed to debate and vote on all subjects. Though this time Gladstone did consider rather more carefully the problem of Ulster, in the end no special arrangements were made for the province.

The Second Home Rule Bill was introduced by Gladstone in the House of Commons in February 1893 in an impressive speech. The debate that followed was as furious as ever – though the arguments were much the same on either side as in 1886. In the end the Bill was passed on its Second Reading in September by 43 votes (347 to 304); 'too small, too small', Gladstone murmured perceptively. Within less than a week it was rejected by the massive majority of 419 to 41 in the House of Lords. The Lords implicitly justified their action by pointing to the lack of an English majority in favour of Home Rule, since (excluding the Irish MPs) the Home Rulers in the House of Commons were in a minority. Gladstone accepted the defeat philosophically. He carried on as Prime Minister for another seven months, increasingly at odds with his Cabinet colleagues, until his final reluctant retirement in March 1894. He died four years later.

Gladstone's personal and obsessive commitment to Home Rule after the summer of 1885 led him to underestimate – indeed to ignore – the problems involved in getting such a measure accepted. Not only was there a great deal of anti-Irish and anti-Catholic feeling among the English electors, there was considerably more opposition to his policy within the Liberal Party than the Prime Minister expected. Yet the signs had been there for some time. By the early 1880s many Whigs were already worried by the implications of Gladstone's Irish land policy for the rights of property generally, and a number had already abandoned the Liberal Party. For some Radicals such as Joseph Chamberlain Home Rule seemed the very antithesis of their commitment to strong, efficient, progressive government within an imperial framework.

An even more formidable obstacle to Home Rule was the House of Lords with its built-in Unionist majority, as Gladstone himself had realised by his willingness in 1885 to allow Salisbury to initiate that policy. As the fate of his own 1893 Bill showed, it was virtually certain that any Home Rule Bill would be destroyed by the House of Lords. To continue with it under those circumstances seemed to many Liberals – even devoted Gladstonians – sheer perversity. It meant the sacrifice of the unity and future prospects of the Liberal Party to an old man's pride and stubbornness. One result of the bill's failure, however, was to convince Gladstone and most Liberals that reform of the House of Lords was a necessary prelude to any future radical programme.

Historians writing within the Liberal tradition, such as J.L. Hammond, have implied that a great opportunity for settling the Irish question was lost when parliament rejected Home Rule. That may be so. Yet recent historians have stressed the enormous problems that would have arisen in implementing it. They have pointed to the complexity of the financial provisions of the Bills; the difficulties involved in the division of powers between the Irish and the Imperial parliaments; the persistence of extremist forms of nationalism; and, above all, the opposition of Protestant Ulster to rule from Dublin.

Nevertheless, despite Gladstone's failure, the commitment to Irish Home Rule remained an integral part of the Party's programme. As we see in the next chapter, the Liberals returned to power in 1905 and introduced a Third Home Rule Bill in 1912. Even from the grave, therefore, the long arm of Gladstone reached out to shape Liberal policy.

Summary Diagram

Gladstone, Parnell and Home Rule

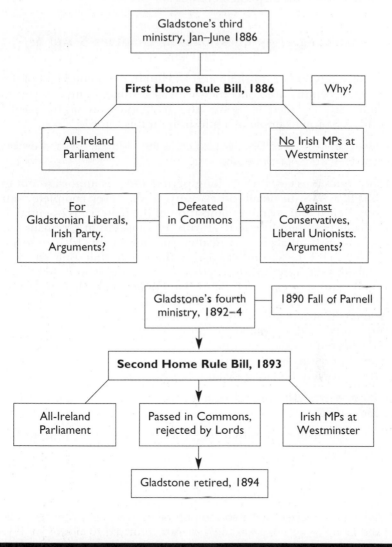

Gladstone's third ministry, Jan–June 1886

First Home Rule Bill, 1886 — Why?

All-Ireland Parliament

No Irish MPs at Westminster

For
Gladstonian Liberals,
Irish Party.
Arguments?

Defeated in Commons

Against
Conservatives,
Liberal Unionists.
Arguments?

Gladstone's fourth ministry, 1892–4

1890 Fall of Parnell

Second Home Rule Bill, 1893

All-Ireland Parliament

Passed in Commons, rejected by Lords

Irish MPs at Westminster

Gladstone retired, 1894

Working on Chapter 6

You need to make detailed notes on Gladstone's Home Rule policy. This is a long and complicated topic, in which key details – such as the differences between the first and second Home Rule Bills – are of the first importance, and it is essential to get them right. In addition, you must explain clearly why Gladstone came to support Home Rule; the arguments for and against; and the consequences of his policies. Also, you should draw on this chapter and the last to outline Parnell's career and to list his major achievements.

Answering essay questions on Chapters 5 and 6

Most questions on Great Britain and Ireland in the second half of the nineteenth century are concerned with Gladstone. Many ask you to explain why he failed to 'solve' the Irish question or to 'pacify' Ireland. A typical example of a question on this topic is:

1 Assess the efforts of Gladstone to solve the Irish question and explain why they were not more successful.

All such questions cover a very long period and it is important not to get bogged down in detail, otherwise you will never complete your answer. A clear and cogent organisation of the material is essential. It is probably best therefore to deal with the question in two main sections: the first analysing critically the period of Irish reforms (1868–82); and the second discussing the Home Rule Bills and why they failed. One approach to Gladstone's 'failure' is to differentiate between reasons relating to Ireland (land policy? Parnell?), and those relating to Great Britain (party politics? Ulster?).

You could also expect a question on Parnell's career and achievements. Some of the problems relating to this type of question have already been discussed in connection with O'Connell (see page 50).

Some questions on this period are concerned with the effects of the Irish problem on Great Britain. For example:

2 What effects did the Irish question have on British party politics 1867–1886?

What are the major issues that ought to be discussed in your answer to this question?

As with the earlier nineteenth century, more general, long-term questions are also often asked on the later period, and sometimes they go up to 1914. A typical question is:

3 What factors prevented a solution of the Irish problem between 1886 and 1914?

A chronological approach to such a question would be quite inappropriate. Instead, you need to look at the period as a whole, seize upon a small number of key issues (as in structured questions) and build up an answer around them.

Source-based questions on Chapter 6

1 The First Home Rule Bill 1886

Read the extract from Gladstone's speech on page 97, and look at the cartoon on page 98. Answer the following questions.

a) Why did Gladstone feel that, over Home Rule, 'a tory government can do it more easily and safely than any other'? (*4 marks*)

b) Explain briefly why in fact the task of implementing Home Rule fell upon Gladstone in January 1886. (*6 marks*)

c) Why did Gladstone insist at the outset, in introducing his Home Rule Bill, that he had no intention of proposing the repeal of the Union? (*5 marks*)

d) In relation to this extract, why did Gladstone feel justified in ignoring the views of Ulster? (*4 marks*)

e) Why, as in the cartoon, did many political observers regard Gladstone's First Home Rule Bill as a 'Great Liberal Cabinet trick'? (*6 marks*)

f) What were Gladstone's real motives in introducing the First Home Rule Bill? (*10 marks*)

2 Parnell

Read Gladstone's letter on page 100 and Davitt's description on page 101. Answer the following questions.

a) In the eyes of Gladstone what were the 'splendid services' rendered by Parnell to his country before 1890? (*6 marks*)

b) Why did Gladstone believe that Parnell's continuation as Irish Party leader after 1890 would be 'disastrous ... to the cause of Ireland'? (*5 marks*)

c) How was he proved correct? (*4 marks*)

d) Why did Gladstone believe that his own leadership of the Liberal Party would be impossible if Parnell continued as Irish leader? (*4 marks*)

e) Davitt suggests that Parnell bore 'no resemblance of any kind' to his predecessors as Irish nationalist leader. Mention briefly some ways in which this was so. (*6 marks*)

f) What were Parnell's main achievements as an Irish leader? (*10 marks*)

7 The Ulster Problem

POINTS TO CONSIDER

In 1912 the Liberals introduced another Home Rule Bill; but, rather than solving the Irish Question, it threatened to unleash civil war. It is essential for you to understand why Home Rule was anathema to the Protestants of Ulster, why there was no simple 'solution' to which the Liberal government could turn, and why the outbreak of the First World War in 1914 merely postponed crisis in Ireland.

KEY DATES

1886	(January) Ulster Repeal Union set up
1900	reunion of Irish Parliamentary Party under John Redmond
1903	Wyndham's Land Act
1905	Ulster Unionist Council formed
1906	(January) Liberal landslide victory at general election
1907	Liberals' Irish Councils Bill dropped
1910	general elections, wiping out Liberal majority; (February) Carson elected leader of Ulster Unionists
1911	Parliament Act abolished Lords' permanent veto
1912	(April) Third Home Rule Bill introduced; (September) Solemn League and Covenant signed
1913	(January) Ulster Volunteer Force (UVF) set up; (November) Irish Volunteers formed
1914	(March) Curragh 'Mutiny'; (April) Larne gun-running incident; (May) Home Rule Bill passed; (July) Home Rule Amending Bill rejected by Lords, Buckingham Palace Conference failed, Howth gun-running incident; (4 August) Britain entered First World War

1 The Origins of Ulster Unionism

KEY ISSUE Why were the Ulster Unionists so vehemently opposed to Home Rule?

Ever since they came to Ireland, centuries before, the Protestants had been marked off by religion and culture from the Catholic majority. Nowhere was this sense of a separate identity stronger than in Ulster, where the majority of Protestants were concentrated. Though they represented only about a quarter of the total Irish population around 1900, the Protestants in Ulster formed about 57 per cent of the people of that province. Protestant separatism in Ulster was sustained not only by the fervour and rabid anti-Papalism of the dominant Presbyterian churches, but also by the nature of the Ulster economy. For Ulster was the only segment of Ireland where – following on from the linen trades of earlier centuries – a truly industrial economy had developed. Ulster thus became not only the most progressive and prosperous province in Ireland, but, owing to its dependence on British markets and raw materials, an area which looked outwards to Great Britain rather than southwards to the rest of Ireland.

In these circumstances it was natural enough that the Ulstermen should have become stalwart defenders of the Union after 1801. After the collapse of the repeal and revolutionary movements in the 1840s, there seemed to be no outstanding threat to the status quo during the relatively quiet years of the mid-nineteenth century. Hence there appeared to be no need for them to take special measures to defend their position. It was not until the 1880s that the Ulster Protestants began to organise in defence of the Union – and as a result Ulster unionism was born.

This was due to the re-emergence of Irish nationalism and the rise of the Home Rule Party in Ireland at that time, followed by the Home Rulers' swift capture of the Roman Catholic vote together with the introduction of Gladstone's Home Rule Bills in 1886 and 1893. These developments, by raising the spectre of self-government for the whole of Ireland centred on a Dublin parliament, seemed to threaten the very existence of the Ulster Protestant way of life. One response to this threat was the revival of the Protestant Orange Order. But political organisation among the Ulster Protestants to defend the Union emerged only slowly. In the key election of 1885, for example, Liberals and Conservatives in northern Ireland still opposed one another, and as a result the Nationalist Party under Parnell won 17 Ulster seats (out of 33) compared with only three in the general election of 1880. It also swept the board in southern Ireland. The shock of these results, together with the introduction of Gladstone's First Home Rule Bill which soon followed, brought members of the most influential Protestant groups in Ulster – landowners, businessmen, churchmen – together in January 1886 in the Loyalist Anti-Repeal Union, in opposition to Home Rule. The movement grew rapidly. It was strengthened by the visit of an up-and-coming Tory politician, Lord Randolph Churchill, to Belfast in February. There Lord Randolph decided (in his own famous phrase) 'to play the Orange card' – to use Ulster unionism to weaken Gladstone's position and advance the interests of his own party. At a large and enthusiastic public meeting he called upon the Ulstermen to organise in opposition to Gladstone and Home Rule, and hinted, ominously, that such resistance would receive support in England: 'Ulster will fight, and Ulster will be right'.

The introduction of the First Home Rule Bill in April 1886 led virtually all the Ulster Liberals to break with their party and join with the Conservatives to denounce the proposal to hand them over 'to their inveterate nationalist foes'. This Conservative-Liberal Unionist alliance was maintained firmly at the general election in the summer of 1886 following the defeat in the Commons of the Home Rule Bill. This time the unionists won just a majority of the Ulster seats – 17 out of 33. Politics in Ulster was now completely polarised between the unionists and the nationalists. The tensions created there by the Home Rule crisis were illustrated by the sectarian riots in the Belfast shipyards that spring, which led to 32 deaths and scores of injuries.

Following the 1886 general election the unionists worked hard to consolidate their forces in Ulster and justify their stance. Unionist clubs were formed throughout the province, links were established with the unionists in the south and with the Conservative Party on the mainland, and a propaganda campaign was carried out in Great Britain on behalf of the Ulster unionist cause. An Ulster Defence Association was also formed – a portent of what was to come.

Why were the Ulster unionists so vehemently opposed to Home Rule? They defended the Union, in the first place, because they believed there were sound economic reasons for doing so. Ireland, they argued, had prospered under the Union: the British connection had helped produce thriving industries in Ulster upon which the prosperity of the whole region was based. That prosperity would be threatened if the link with Britain was broken; especially if, as seemed likely, an Irish parliament introduced a system of protective duties against British goods and raw materials. 'All our progress has been made under the Union,' the Belfast Chamber of Commerce told Gladstone in 1893; 'why should we be driven by force to abandon the conditions which have led to that success?' But southern Ireland, they insisted, had also benefited from the British connection, as revealed by the reforms introduced by successive governments.

Politically too, the Irish unionists were fearful of what the results of an Irish parliament would be. It would, they believed, be dominated by extreme nationalists, radicals and Fenians, who possessed little respect for persons or property and whose ultimate goal was a completely independent Ireland. By opposing Home Rule, therefore, the unionists were at the same time defending the integrity of the Empire. The last point, as always, was the religious one. In the famous unionist phrase: 'Home Rule is Rome Rule'. The Protestants' image of the Roman Catholic Church – based on historical memory and the contemporary links between Irish Catholicism and Irish nationalism – convinced them that their religious and civil liberties would be threatened by a Dublin parliament which would represent an overwhelming Catholic majority.

It must be said that Irish nationalists hardly went out of their way to face up to genuine unionist fears about the consequences of Home Rule. But, equally, the unionists underestimated the emotional force of an Irish nationalism which aimed at unity and freedom for the whole island. Thus, as the twentieth century dawned, there was no real dialogue between the two sides.

The prospect of Home Rule receded after the defeat of the Second Home Rule Bill in 1893 and lifted the immediate danger to Ulster. Gladstone retired the following year, and the Irish Parliamentary Party disintegrated into warring factions following the death of Parnell in 1891. Irish nationalism temporarily became more cultural than political, as with the founding in 1893 of the Gaelic League, which aimed to 'De-Anglicise' Irish culture and revive the use of the Gaelic language. Furthermore the Conservatives triumphed at the general elections of 1895 and 1900. The Conservatives then attempted to 'to kill Home Rule with kindness' by a policy of radical reform in Ireland. The Local Government Act of 1898, which introduced elected County Councils, destroyed the waning power of the landed gentry throughout the country, and handed over local political power ever more firmly to the middle-class unionists in Ulster and their nationalist counterparts in Catholic Ireland. Wyndham's Act of 1903 (named after the Irish Secretary) more or less solved the land problem in Ireland by organising the buying out of the landlords by the state at an acceptable price, and allowing their tenants to purchase their lands through state loans at a very low rate of interest extended over a long period.

Yet the relationship between the Ulster unionists and the Conservative government was not all sweetness and light. In 1904 a devolution scheme was produced behind-the-scenes at the Irish Office, which proposed the control of some important aspects of Irish internal affairs, including finance, by a representative Irish Council. This was denounced by the Ulster unionists when the details leaked out as 'Home Rule by instalments'. It led to their increasing distrust of the government, even though the scheme was repudiated by the Prime Minister, A.J. Balfour, and George Wyndham was forced to resign. The eventual outcome of this political storm in a teacup, however, was vitally important and represents (in the words of the historian George Boyce) 'one of the most significant events in the political history of modern Ireland'. It led directly to the formation of the Ulster Unionist Council in March 1905, centred on Belfast: a democratically elected body which now represented every strand of Ulster unionism – the unionist clubs, the Orange Order, the Protestant churches and the Ulster members of the Commons and Lords. The Council thus became the directing force of Ulster unionism, and therefore in any future political crisis Ulster unionism could speak with one powerful, unified voice. Even more portentously, it also meant that Ulster now possessed the framework of an independent governmental organisation, which could be summoned into life as and when the political situation demanded.

2 The Liberals and Home Rule, 1900–12

> **KEY ISSUE** For what reasons, and with what success, did the
> Liberals introduce a third Home Rule Bill?

a) The Liberals and Home Rule to 1911

Though the Liberal Party after 1900 remained committed in principle to Home Rule for Ireland, important sections of the party
regarded it as an irritating distraction, diverting energies away from
more urgent plans for imperial and social reconstruction. The new
party leader, Sir Henry Campbell-Bannerman, and his Chief Whip,
Herbert Gladstone, saw their main task as the reorganisation and re-
unification of the Liberal Party. They were well aware of the lessons of
the disastrous general election of 1895 which had given the Tories
their greatest electoral victory of the nineteenth century, and they
attributed this mainly to the unpopularity in England of Irish Home
Rule. What the party leaders wanted was a more practical and less
ideological approach to the issue, especially as they realised, realistically, that Home Rule was impossible while the House of Lords
retained its traditional powers. Moreover, as the decline of the
Conservative government under Balfour became more evident in the
early years of the new century, the desire for Liberal unity to prepare
for the coming general election became paramount. All sections of
the Liberal Party therefore accepted Campbell-Bannerman's formula,
adopted early in 1905, of a 'step by step' approach to the Irish question. Irish reform, yes; but (in Herbert Gladstone's phrase) 'no
pledge either as to method or time' over Home Rule.

During the election campaign of 1906, therefore, the issue of
Home Rule was played down, and the Liberal Party leaders made it
clear that if elected there would be no early introduction of Home
Rule. After the Liberals' landslide victory that year (which gave them
400 MPs and an overall majority of 270), all that the Irish were offered
in 1907 was another Councils Bill which aimed at introducing administrative devolution. This was merely a revised version of the Unionist
bill of 1904 and proposed a representative Irish Council to deal with
some aspects of Irish internal affairs. It was rejected out of hand by
John Redmond, the moderate leader of the Irish Parliamentary Party.
Even apart from his own views, Redmond was under pressure from
the extremists within his own party and the new nationalist organisation, Sinn Fein (see page 133), to stand firm over Irish demands.
Thus, it was now made crystal clear to the Liberal government that
half measures would not suffice – nothing less than Home Rule would
be acceptable.

Yet there was little that the Irish Parliamentary Party could do to
bring pressure to bear on the government. The Liberals had a mass-

ive parliamentary majority, and (especially after Asquith replaced Campbell-Bannerman as Prime Minister in 1908) most of their time and energy went into promoting the radical social welfare programme which was their major achievement on the domestic front. It is true that the government was determined to deal with the problem of the House of Lords (which had rejected a number of Liberal bills passed by the Commons), but Asquith did not feel that Home Rule was the most popular issue on which to challenge the Lords' powers. For the moment, therefore, the Irish had to bide their time, though Redmond still believed – in opposition to some of his nationalist compatriots – that support for the Liberals offered the best hope for Home Rule.

The whole situation was changed dramatically when the Lords in an act of suicidal folly rejected Lloyd George's 'People's Budget' in November 1909. They objected particularly to the proposed new super tax and taxes on land values, and were driven to desperation by the witty, taunting speeches directed against them by the Chancellor of the Exchequer. But by long constitutional practice the Lords had no right to reject a 'money bill' passed by the Commons. The unwise Lords' action – which brought to a head years of Liberal anger and frustration over their blatantly partisan behaviour – made the reform of the powers of the Upper House inevitable.

The rejection of the Budget was followed by the dissolution of parliament and a general election to be held in January 1910. For Redmond, the Irish leader, this seemed to offer new opportunities for the cause of Home Rule, for he believed that the Liberals would need Irish support at the hustings. And if another Liberal victory in 1910 was followed by the expected reform of the Lords, then there would be no legitimate obstacle to the introduction of a new Home Rule Bill.

Redmond's views were conveyed to Asquith in a letter the Irish leader wrote to the veteran Home Ruler, John Morley, in November 1909.

1 The political conditions in Ireland are such that unless an official declaration on the question of home rule be made, not only will it be impossible for us to support Liberal candidates in England, but we will ... have to ask our friends [Irish voters] to vote against them ... We
5 cannot acquiesce in the present situation being continued. There is a large majority in the government and in the House of Commons in favour of home rule and yet their hands are tied ... We must, therefore, press for an official declaration which will show clearly that the home rule issue is involved in the issue of the House of Lords by declar-
10 ing that the government shall be free to deal with it, not on the lines of the Council Bill, but on the lines of national self government, subject to imperial control, in the next parliament.

Though it was not the only factor affecting Asquith's election campaign in 1909–10, the Prime Minister heeded Redmond's warning. For the Liberal leadership the election was centred on the major issue of ending the absolute veto of the House of Lords over legislation, and to achieve this Asquith needed the support of all the anti-Conservative forces in the country. Hence, in his great speech at the Albert Hall on 10 December 1909, the Prime Minister made in effect a definite commitment to introduce a Home Rule Bill in the next parliament if the Liberals were re-elected, as well as promising to deal with the grievances of other disaffected groups whose claims had been rejected by the House of Lords.

However, the outcome of the general election of January 1910 was a disappointment for the Liberals in that their majority over the Conservatives was wiped out and they were reduced to the same number of MPs as their opponents. But Asquith was able to carry on as Prime Minister with firm support from the Irish and the Labour Party. In June the Commons passed by a substantial majority the government's Parliament Bill, and the Lords then, resignedly, passed the Budget. But it took another general election (in December 1910), which was virtually a re-enactment of the first, before the Lords agreed to bow to the will of the House of Commons and pass the Parliament Bill, which they did in August 1911. The Parliament Act of 1911 abolished the absolute veto of the House of Lords over legislation, and ensured that the Upper House could only hold up a bill passed formally by the House of Commons for two years (three successive parliamentary sessions). In this way the long-drawn-out constitutional crisis came to an end. The Irish could now look forward to the introduction of a new Home Rule Bill.

b) The Home Rule Bill, 1912

The Liberal government introduced its Home Rule Bill in the following year. The state of the parties in the House of Commons (following the general election of December 1910) was now: Liberals 272; Unionists 272 (including 16 Ulster Unionists); Irish Nationalists 84; and Labour 42. It has been argued by many historians that the Liberals' introduction of the Home Rule Bill was due to pressure from the Irish Nationalists and their reliance on Irish votes in the House of Commons to maintain the government in power. Patricia Jalland, however, in her detailed study of the Liberals and Ireland during this period, has insisted that Liberal policy was, on the contrary, 'the logical consequence of a long-standing commitment'. Liberal leaders since the days of Gladstone's last ministry had consistently supported Irish Home Rule in principle. Augustine Birrell, the Irish Secretary, had told Redmond, the Irish Nationalist leader, a year before the elections of 1910 had drastically cut down the Liberal majority, that Home Rule was 'the live policy of the Party without limitation or restriction'. In any case, she argues, the Liberal government was not dependent on Irish votes, since if both Irish Nationalist and Irish Unionist votes were excluded from the reckoning, the government had a small majority of 16 over the Conservatives – which would normally be increased to over 50 with the support of Labour. Thus, Jalland concludes, only an overwhelming belief by the Liberal Party that, for the sake of honour and conviction, it must attempt to secure Home Rule for Ireland, can explain why over the next two years it was prepared to endure the storms and stresses of another and greater Home Rule crisis.

The Home Rule Bill of 1912 was fundamentally the same as Gladstone's of 1893, and it was a very moderate measure. There was to be an Irish parliament, consisting of a small, nominated Senate (Upper House) and an elected House of Commons. The Executive would be responsible to parliament. The powers of the Irish parliament were to be even more limited than those proposed in 1893, since the Imperial government (in addition to its retention of the major powers listed in the 1893 bill) was now to have a greater degree of financial control over Ireland and would also be responsible for the new old age pensions and national insurance schemes. Ireland was also to be represented at Westminster by 42 MPs. The main point about the new bill, however, was that once again Ulster was to be included in a self-governing Ireland. This was due not only to the pull of the past; self-deception and complacency also played a part. There was little real discussion of the Ulster problem among Liberals, whether in Cabinet, the House of Commons or even in the columns of the Liberal press, despite the fact that the Ulster unionists had insisted for over a year that they would resist the implementation of Home Rule. Many Liberals had convinced themselves that unionist opposition was somehow 'artificial'.

Asquith bears a major responsibility for this. He more or less controlled Irish policy after 1911, and his prevarication and refusal to take hard decisions, as well as the influence of Redmond (who declared that 'Irish Nationalists can never be consenting parties to the mutilation of the Irish nation'), meant that there was no real attempt to face up to the realities of the Ulster situation at the outset, when a compromise solution was perhaps possible. By 1914, the situation had deteriorated so much that almost any compromise scheme was bound to fail. 'This failure to assess the Ulster problem', writes Jalland, 'and to examine the possible methods of dealing with it, is surely a severe indictment of the Government'. On the other hand, Asquith's biographer, Roy Jenkins (both an historian and an experienced politician) believes that Ulster unionist intransigence and Redmond's need to maintain his credibility as an Irish nationalist leader made a settlement no more likely in 1912 than in 1914.

The Home Rule Bill was introduced by Asquith in the House of Commons in April 1912 in an eloquent speech, directed at the opposition.

1 We put this Bill forward as ... the embodiment of our own honest and
deliberate judgement. What is your alternative? Are you satisfied with
the present system? ... What do you propose to put in its place? Have
you any answer to the demand of Ireland beyond the naked veto of an
5 irreconcilable minority and the promise of a freer and more copious
outflow to Ireland of Imperial doles? There are at this moment between
twenty and thirty self-governing Legislatures under the allegiance of the
Crown. They have solved ... the problem of reconciling local autonomy
with Imperial unity. Are we going to break up the Empire by adding one
10 more?

Despite the limited powers granted to the Irish parliament, Redmond
and the Nationalist Party gave Asquith strong support.

The Conservatives, however, were determined to kill the bill, come
what may. They were now led by Andrew Bonar Law, a Scots-Canadian
industrialist, who had succeeded Balfour as Conservative leader in
November 1911. Law was (or appeared to be) a much tougher character than the fastidious Balfour; he had grown up in Ulster (where
his father had been a Presbyterian minister) and this made him particularly sympathetic to the claims and outlook of the Ulster unionists.
Law attacked the Home Rule Bill on the grounds that it was the outcome of a 'corrupt bargain' between Asquith and Redmond – the
price to be paid for gaining Irish votes to prop up the government –
and besides, he argued, the Liberals had no mandate to introduce
Home Rule (as the recent election campaign had shown), nor any
real enthusiasm for the project. These, perhaps largely specious, arguments were ignored by the supporters of Home Rule, but so too were
the powerful points produced by the leaders of the Ulster unionists
on behalf of their province. The bill easily passed through the
Commons at the end of May 1912 with a majority of about 100.

But the Commons' vote meant little since, as everyone realised, the
bill would certainly be rejected by the House of Lords – as it was by an
enormous majority – and the Lords' opposition could only be overcome by the application of the 1911 Parliament Act. The Bill could
not therefore become law before the spring of 1914 at the earliest.
This two-year wait was bound to increase all the tensions and bitterness surrounding the issue; on one notorious occasion in the House
of Commons Asquith was howled down by the opposition. It also
encouraged extremism in Ulster. This meant that the fate of the bill
would be decided by events outside parliament, and indeed the
Liberal government now found itself opposed by the united, stubborn
resistance of the Ulster unionists, prepared to push their opposition
– as the formation of the Ulster Volunteers soon showed – to the
point of armed revolt.

3 Ulster Resistance

> **KEY ISSUE** In what ways did Unionists justify their resistance?

Even before the Home Rule Bill was presented to the House of Commons the Ulster Unionist Council had begun to organise resistance. It also put its case to the British people through its own propaganda and the co-operation of the Conservative Party. Two men now emerged as the main leaders of Irish unionist resistance – Sir Edward Carson and James Craig.

Sir Edward Carson was a southern Protestant lawyer, who had been born in Dublin in 1854 and educated there at Trinity College. He had an outstanding career at the Bar in Ireland and England. After his election as Liberal Unionist MP for Dublin University in 1892 he was appointed Solicitor-General for Ireland by Lord Salisbury, and later, in 1900, Solicitor-General for England. By birth and upbringing Carson had little in common with the Ulster unionists; but, as he said, the maintenance of the Union 'is the guiding star of my political life', and he was prepared to use Ulster as a base to prevent any Home Rule Bill. In this way he hoped that the position of the weak and scattered southern unionists would also be protected. In 1910 he was recognised as the leader of the Ulster Unionists in the House of Commons. At his famous visit to Belfast in the following year he proclaimed that Ulster's cause was 'the cause of the Empire', and announced solemnly, 'I dedicate myself to your service whatever may happen'. Carson proved to be a redoubtable advocate of Ulster's claims and a determined supporter of her resistance to Home Rule.

Craig, the son of a Belfast distiller, was by contrast a much more provincial and less commanding figure, though he had fought with distinction in the South African War and had sat in the House of Commons as an Ulster Unionist MP since 1906. He was obstinate and single-minded and determined at all costs to resist any attempt to force Ulster into a self-governing Ireland. Craig's real strength lay in action and administration: it was he who began the organisation of provincial government in Ulster on behalf of the Ulster Council, in order to take over local power if Home Rule became law. It was Craig too who first began to speak in terms of armed resistance to Home Rule.

For the moment, however, resistance took the form of great meetings and military-type demonstrations embracing all classes and groups in Protestant Ulster, to express their determination to oppose Home Rule. Typical of these actions was the great protest demonstration organised in Belfast's Balmoral grounds on Easter Tuesday 1912, two days before Asquith introduced the Home Rule Bill in the House of Commons. There an estimated 100,000 Ulstermen marched past the platform, where Bonar Law and Carson were present as the main speakers, together with 70 British Conservative MPs. The culmination of this provocative movement to display the solidarity and resolution of Protestant Ulster was the nomination by the Ulster Unionist Council of 28 September 1912 as 'Covenant Day' and a public holiday. Ulster's 'Solemn League and Covenant' (see below) was then signed by about a quarter-of-a-million men. Carson signed first; some men (it is reported) signed with their own blood. A similar declaration was supported by roughly the same number of women.

ULSTER'S SOLEMN LEAGUE AND COVENANT

Being convinced in our consciences that Home Rule would be disastrous to the material well-being of Ulster, as well as of the whole of Ireland, subversive of our civil and religious freedom, destructive of our citizenship, and perilous to the unity of the Empire, we, whose names are underwritten, men of Ulster, loyal subjects of his Glorious Majesty King George V, humbly relying on the God Whom our fathers ... confidently trusted, do hereby pledge ourselves in solemn Covenant throughout this our time of threatened calamity to stand by one another in defending ... our cherished position of equal citizenship in the United Kingdom and in using all means which may be found necessary to defeat the present conspiracy to set up a home rule parliament in Ireland. And in the event of such a Parliament being forced upon us we further and mutually pledge ourselves to refuse to recognise its authority. In sure confidence that God will defend the right.

The implication of the Ulstermen's determination to defend themselves was seen shortly after the signing of the Covenant. Sporadic drilling and training of volunteer soldiers had been taking place for some time (with the acquiescence of the local Protestant JPs), and these men were now organised by the Ulster Unionist Council into the Ulster Volunteer Force (UVF). In setting up the force the Council received the advice of Field-Marshal Lord Roberts; and a retired British officer, Lieutenant-General Sir George Richardson, was appointed as Commanding Officer. The Ulster Volunteer Force grew rapidly and was organised into county divisions and regiments throughout the province, backed up by supporting corps of nurses, despatch riders etc. Most of the men in the new force did not possess arms, and those who did were for the moment not allowed to display them. The UVF, however, was almost certainly an illegal organisation, yet it was supported by MPs such as Carson and Craig who soon made it clear that they were prepared to use force to resist subjection to a Dublin parliament. Why were the Ulster unionists prepared to push their opposition to Home Rule to such lengths?

A postcard of 1912, which appeals to the British not to sever economic and political ties with Ulster.

The Ulstermen took their stand on their established constitutional and legal rights. They argued that they were justified in defying a law which overrode the rights of minorities, especially a minority so united in its resistance to the dictates of the government. Moreover, no safeguards were provided for their religious or civil liberties within the Home Rule Bill to which they were being asked to submit – a bill which many Irish nationalists were already describing as merely 'a provisional settlement'. Irish self-government, therefore, might well lead on to independence. 'We see', said Carson, 'that there can be no permanent resting place between complete union and total separation.' Thus the integrity of the Empire was also at stake. The unionists concluded, therefore, that their duty to the Crown, as the symbol of Imperial unity and constitutional authority, was greater than their duty to the law passed by a particular government.

Bonar Law was sympathetic to these claims. He had spoken at the great Balmoral meeting in Belfast on Easter Tuesday 1912; and at a speech in July of that year at a mass meeting held at Blenheim Palace, he appeared to go even further and give full endorsement to any resistance measures planned by the Ulster unionists.

1   In our opposition ... we shall not be guided by the considerations or
    bound by the restraints which would influence us in an ordinary con-
    stitutional struggle ... if an attempt were made to deprive these men
    [Ulster unionists] of their birth-right – as part of a corrupt parliamen-
5   tary bargain – they would be justified in resisting such an attempt by all

means in their power, including force ... if such an attempt is made, I can imagine no length of resistance to which Ulster can go in which I should not be prepared to support them, and in which, in my belief, they would not be supported by the overwhelming majority of the
10 British people.

Such sentiments did not mean that Bonar Law and the Conservative Party supported the Ulster unionists' claims for the sake of Ulster: what moved them were primarily Imperial and – it must be said – party considerations. Ulster unionist resistance would help the Conservatives destroy the Home Rule Bill and thus preserve the integrity of the United Kingdom and the Empire. At the same time, the destruction of the Home Rule Bill might well bring down in its wake the hated Liberal government.

4 1914: Year of Crisis

> **KEY ISSUES** Was civil war averted only by the First World War?

The belligerent speeches of Unionist leaders such as Carson and Law were denounced by Asquith as a 'Grammar of Anarchy'. But anarchy was a subject which a statesman such as Asquith – moderate, rational, legalistic – could neither comprehend nor master. 'I tell you quite frankly', he told a public meeting in Dublin in July 1912, 'I do not believe in the prospect of a civil war'. Redmond, similarly, assured him that the unionists were playing 'a gigantic game of bluff and blackmail'. It is true that the Ulster Volunteer Force was intended in the first place to be a powerful pressure group to force the Liberal government to give way peacefully over Home Rule; but all the evidence points to the fact that, if the testing time came, Ulster would fight. Faced then with intransigence and subversion by the unionists both at Belfast and Westminster, and unable or unwilling to impose a more compromising policy upon his Irish nationalist allies, Asquith adopted his old policy of 'Wait and See'. No action was to be taken against the spokesmen for rebellion. By a display of 'massive calmness' (in Roy Jenkins' admiring phrase), and the conviction that the Irish question still remained amenable to a parliamentary solution, the Prime Minister hoped to bring his opponents to their senses.

Yet the ultimate effect of the policy of 'drift' was to exacerbate rather than relieve the growing tensions in Ireland. In November 1913, following the example of the UVF in Ulster, a group of republicans and moderate nationalists in the south founded the Irish Volunteers as a defence force. This grew rapidly throughout Catholic Ireland and was eventually supported by Redmond and the Irish Parliamentary Party. By 1914, therefore, the government was faced with private armies in the north and the south; but Asquith did nothing, though action against Ulster was urged by some of the more belligerent members of the Cabinet, notably Winston Churchill, First Lord of the Admiralty.

The government's position was weakened even further by the so-called Curragh 'Mutiny' in March 1914. This incident arose from the government's decision to reinforce the army depots in Ulster – where some 23,000 men were now enrolled in the UVF, faced by only about 1,000 regular troops. This led to rumours among the unionists that the army was to be used to 'invade' Ulster and crush the UVF, though the government had no such clear-cut plans. In this situation the War Office became worried about the loyalty of officers stationed in Ireland who came from Ulster. A message was therefore sent to the Commanding Officer in Ireland, indicating that in the event of hostilities officers from Ulster would be allowed to be 'absent from duty' and should 'disappear from Ireland'. On the other hand, if other officers were not prepared to carry out orders they would be 'be dismissed from the Service'. As a result of the War Office's foolishness in posing such hypothetical issues, and the bungling way in which the message was delivered to the officers assembled at the army headquarters at the Curragh, in County Kildare, General Gough and 57 officers of the Cavalry Brigade said they preferred dismissal. The British public was appalled by the what the press called a 'mutiny', and as a result of the recriminations that followed, the War Minister, Colonel Seely, was forced to resign. The Curragh 'Mutiny' convinced Asquith that it would be impossible to take military action against Ulster. There is no doubt, he wrote, that 'if we were to order a march upon Ulster about half the officers in the Army ... would strike ... That is the present situation and it is not a pleasant one'.

The shock waves produced by the Curragh 'Mutiny' had hardly died down, when news came in the following month of the Larne gun-running incident. On the night of 24–5 April 1914, in a daring and completely successful operation which defied the ban on importing arms, the UVF obtained 35,000 rifles and 5 million rounds of ammunition from Germany. They were landed at Larne, on the north-east coast, and collected by the Volunteers' Motor Car Corps – under the noses of the authorities – and quietly distributed throughout the province. The nationalists were outraged. The government was left demoralised. 'It was no longer a question of our coercing Ulster', said one Liberal minister; 'it was a question of our preventing Ulster from coercing us'. Asquith felt he had little choice but to seek a political settlement which gave at least some recognition to Ulster's claims. As Patricia Jalland has commented: 'He relied throughout on a high-risk policy of prevarication and delay which had clearly failed by May 1914'. The outlines of such a settlement had already been put forward by a number of Cabinet minis-

ters before the crises in the spring of 1914. Churchill had written to
Redmond in August 1913:

1   I do not believe there is any real feeling against home rule in the Tory
    party apart from the Ulster question, but they hate the government, are
    bitterly desirous of turning it out, and see in the resistance of Ulster an
    extra-parliamentary force which they will not hesitate to use to the full
5   ... my general view is just what I told you earlier in the year – namely,
    that something should be done to afford the characteristically
    Protestant and Orange counties the option of a moratorium of several
    years before acceding to the Irish parliament ... Much is to be appre-
    hended from ... the fanaticism of these stubborn and determined
10 Orangemen.

This policy of 'exclusion', as it came to be called – that is, excluding
Ulster from a self-governing Ireland – had much to commend it to all
parties by the spring of 1914. Public opinion in Britain seemed to
approve, since such a settlement would recognise the special position
of Ulster without denying the Irish majority Home Rule. Carson and
Craig too realised by this time that a Home Rule Bill for Ireland could
not be stopped, and were therefore prepared to support exclusion in
principle, even though Carson accepted, unhappily, that this meant
deserting the southern unionists. Even Redmond in the end, though
it went against the grain, was prepared to consider a temporary exclusion of the distinctly Protestant areas of Ulster. The application of the
policy of exclusion was, however, much more difficult than it seemed,
since Ulster was not – despite the rhetoric of the unionists – a
Protestant province in toto. Only four counties (see the map on page
10) had definite Protestant majorities: Armagh, Londonderry, Down
and Antrim. In Fermanagh and Tyrone the Protestants and Catholics
were almost evenly divided, and in Cavan, Donegal and Monaghan
the Protestants were in a minority. The problem therefore arose of
what parts of Ulster should be excluded from Home Rule. This was
linked with a second question: if exclusion for some counties was
agreed upon, was it to be temporary or permanent?

    In the end Asquith came to accept 'exclusion' as a reasonable com-
promise plan for both nationalists and unionists, and also as a way out
of his difficulties. In March 1914 an Amending Bill to the original
Home Rule Bill was drawn up based on the principle of 'county
option'. This meant that through a simple majority vote, the electors
in each of the counties of Ulster could decide separately either for or
against exclusion. In addition (as a sop to the Nationalists) those
counties which opted for exclusion were only to be excluded, temporarily, for six years. Whether they were to be allowed to remain permanently outside the rest of a self-governing Ireland would depend
on the verdict of the whole electorate of the United Kingdom at a subsequent general election. Yet the plan was dismissed by Carson as
merely 'a stay of execution' for the Ulster unionists; what he wanted

was an immediate 'clean break' for the whole province of Ulster. Asquith's hopes for an early settlement were in any case destroyed by the House of Lords, which rejected his Amending Bill when it was presented to them in June, and replaced 'county option' by their own Amendment which insisted (like Carson) on the permanent exclusion of the whole province of Ulster.

Once again therefore there appeared to be deadlock. Civil war indeed loomed nearer, since in May the original Home Rule Bill had passed through all the parliamentary stages for it to become law. It was likely, therefore, that the Ulster unionists would carry out their threats to take over the administration of Ulster and defend themselves with the support of the UVF, whose members were now authorised to carry their arms openly. Tensions increased even more when at the end of July the nationalist Volunteers carried out their own gun-running operation in broad daylight at Howth, near Dublin. This was less successful than the UVF's earlier coup at Larne, and, partly owing to the confusion of the authorities, there was a clash between the regular troops and the Volunteers which led to three civilian deaths. The nationalists were furious.

One last effort was made through the king to bring about an agreement, by inviting all the party leaders to a conference at Buckingham Palace on 21 July to discuss 'exclusion'. Though it was generally accepted there that the four 'Protestant' counties should be excluded, there was no agreement at all over the future of Tyrone and Fermanagh, the two counties where there was no clear-cut religious majority. As a result the Buckingham Palace Conference broke up in failure after three days without discussing any other problem. Nevertheless, it is fair to suggest that the principle of the partition of Ireland had been accepted by all sides – and that was to be important for the future.

With the worsening international situation in Europe, Asquith now agreed, at the prompting of all the other party leaders and in the interests of national unity, to abandon his attempt to introduce a revised Amending Bill. Everything was 'put into the shade' (as he wrote to a friend) by the coming war. For the moment the Irish problem was shelved

Summary Diagram

The Ulster Problem

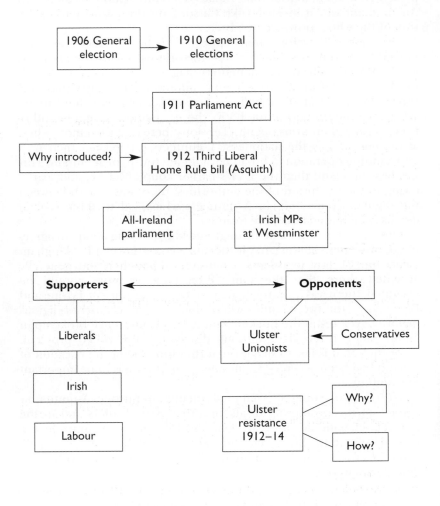

Working on Chapter 7

Your notes should be organised around three major themes: (1) the Home Rule Bill of 1912 (why was it introduced and why were its terms so similar to those in 1893?) (2) the opposition of the Ulster Unionists and the Conservatives, and (3) the Liberal government's reaction to that opposition.

Answering structured and essay questions on Chapter 7

A typical structured question is as follows:

1 **a)** What were the main reasons why the Ulster Unionists opposed Home Rule?
   b) Describe the main provisions of the 1912 Home Rule Bill.
   c) In what ways did the Ulster Unionists oppose this Bill?
   An essay question might take this form:
2 Why, and with what results, was Ulster so bitterly opposed to the Liberals' policy of Home Rule, 1912–14?

Remember to concentrate on analysis rather than narrative. That will involve breaking a large issue into smaller, more manageable ones. In fact, the essay question is very like a summation of the shorter, structured questions.

Source-based questions on Chapter 7

1 The Third Home Rule Bill 1912
Read the extracts from Redmond's letter on pages 113 and Asquith's speech on page 116, and answer the following questions.

a) What were the 'political conditions' in Ireland that Redmond refers to? (*6 marks*)
b) Why did he believe that, as far as the supporters of Home Rule in the government and Commons were concerned, 'their hands are tied'? (*4 marks*)
c) What can we learn from this letter about Redmond's aims as an Irish nationalist leader? (*5 marks*)
d) What can we infer from Asquith's speech about the reasons why he supported a new Home Rule Bill? (*5 marks*)
e) With reference to this speech, why did Asquith support Home Rule for all Ireland? (*5 marks*)

2 Ulster Resistance
Read the Solemn League and Covenant on page 118 and look at the cartoon on page 119. Answer the following questions.

a) Why was the Declaration described as 'Ulster's Solemn League and Covenant'? (*3 marks*)
b) Why did the signatories of the Covenant emphasise that they were 'loyal subjects' of King George V ? (*3 marks*)
c) What did they mean by 'the present conspiracy' in favour of Home Rule? (4 marks)
d) What was significant about the reference to 'using all means' to defend Ulster? (*4 marks*)

e) With reference to the cartoon, why did the Ulster Unionists believe that Home Rule would be disastrous for Ulster? (*6 marks*)

f) How realistic were the fears that led Ulstermen to take up such a firm position by 1912? (*10 marks*)

3 *The Conservative Party and Ulster*

Read the extracts from Bonar Law on pages 119–20, and Churchill on page 122. Answer the following questions.

a) Why did Law argue that the struggle over the Home Rule Bill was not 'an ordinary constitutional struggle'? (*4 marks*)

b) What did he mean by the 'corrupt parliamentary bargain'? (*4 marks*)

c) Why did Bonar Law personally adopt so extremist a position in defence of Ulster? (*3 marks*)

d) Churchill refers to 'a moratorium' on the Protestant counties of Ulster joining in with Home Rule. Why was this suggestion rejected by the Ulster Unionists before 1914? (*4 marks*)

e) How far do the words of Bonar Law and Churchill represent the positions of their two parties? (*5 marks*)

f) Were there realistic hopes of compromise between the Liberal and Conservative parties in 1914? (*10 marks*)

8
The Making of the Anglo-Irish Settlement of 1920–2

POINTS TO CONSIDER

This chapter focuses on what is in many ways the climax to the Irish Question: the bloody Anglo-Irish war of 1919–21 and the Anglo-Irish Settlement of 1921–2. The background to these events needs to be carefully investigated, especially the way in which the Easter Rising led to an escalation of nationalism in Ireland. You also need to be aware of the constraints on Lloyd George, especially the fact that his government was dominated by Conservatives who insisted that Ireland should not become a republic and that the position of the Ulster had to be safe-guarded. It also should be appreciated how this 'answer' to the Irish Question led to further troubles.

KEY DATES

1 Ireland and the First World War

> **KEY ISSUE** Why did Irish Nationalist support for Britain's war effort begin to evaporate?

Ireland's future was now determined more by the impact of the First World War than by any other factor. Britain's declaration of war on Germany on 4 August 1914 was supported both by the Irish Nationalist Party and the Ulster Unionists. Indeed Redmond offered to use the nationalist-controlled Irish Volunteers to help defend the shores of Ireland against enemy action. In return for their patriotic stance both sides hoped to secure some positive response by the British government in support of their Irish claims. Indeed Redmond regarded it as a triumph for the Nationalists when in September Asquith placed the 1914 Irish Home Rule Act on the statute book, though its provisions were to be suspended until the end of the war. No one expected the war to last very long, and so the Unionists in the House of Commons were outraged by what they considered to be Asquith's double-dealing. They acquiesced for the sake of national unity.

In Ireland itself the early period of the war was marked by massive recruiting for the armed forces, both in the north and the south. By the spring of 1916 about 150,000 Irishmen were in active service. There was also increased prosperity, owing to the stimulus given to the Irish economy by the needs of war – especially the demand for foodstuffs – and the money sent home by Irish servicemen. But for Irish nationalists frustration soon set in. As the war dragged on with no sign of an early victory, the prospect of any rapid change in the constitutional status of Ireland became increasingly remote: Home Rule became 'a cheque continuously post-dated'. Even loyal nationalists were irritated by the insensitivity of the British government – by the formation of a special division in the British army for the Ulster Volunteer Force, for example, but not for the Irish Volunteers, and, even more damning, by the appointment of Carson and other leading Irish Unionists to Asquith's Coalition ministry in May 1915.

Many began to feel that the war was no longer Ireland's concern. Redmond's old policy of alliance with the Liberals seemed to have got him nowhere. After the formation of the Coalition in the spring of 1915 the purpose of the Irish Parliamentary Party became difficult to discern. All this played into the hands of the more extreme Irish nationalists. The revolutionaries were soon to advance to the centre of the stage.

2 The Easter Rebellion, 1916

> **KEY ISSUE** Why did a defeated uprising help the cause of Irish
> nationalism?

a) The Rebellion

From the start the revolutionary Irish nationalists – mainly members
of the Irish Republican Brotherhood (Fenians) – had opposed the
war and the policies of the Irish Parliamentary Party, and did their
best to prevent recruitment and support for the British war effort in
Ireland itself. In September 1914, following an incautious public
speech by John Redmond in which he intimated that the Irish
Volunteers might be allowed to serve overseas as well as in Ireland,
the Volunteer movement split. The overwhelming majority – some
180,000 men – remained loyal to Redmond, and became known as
the 'National Volunteers'. A small, anti-war group of about 11,000
men, under the leadership of Eoin MacNeill, set themselves up as a
separate organisation called the 'Irish Volunteers'. The leaders of the
latter group were mostly romantic revolutionaries, strongly influenced by the literary, historical and religious roots of Irish nationalism – MacNeill himself was a professor of medieval Irish history – and
passionately committed to a free and independent Ireland. Their
main aim now was to gain power in Ireland and, with the support of
the Irish people, proclaim an independent Irish republic. MacNeill
himself, the Volunteers' Chief of Staff, was against a premature uprising: it could have no possible chance of success against the British
forces and would only lead to a reckless waste of life. He preferred to
hold the Volunteer force in reserve as a counter in later negotiations
with the British.

Yet a small group of his MacNeill's fellow commanders and other
revolutionaries were prepared to go ahead with an armed rebellion,
despite the odds. Early in 1916 they began planning for an uprising at
Easter. The key figures were Tom Clarke, Sean MacDermott, Patrick
Pearse – in most ways the outstanding personality in the Easter rebellion of 1916 – and James Connolly. For Pearse, questions of military
success or failure were largely irrelevant: the 'blood sacrifice' – to die
for Ireland – was a noble end in itself and would help to stimulate
Irish national consciousness. 'Bloodshed', he had written earlier, 'is a
cleansing and sanctifying thing ... there are many things more horri-
ble than bloodshed, and slavery is one of them'. Connolly, a Marxist,
and the leader of the tiny Irish Citizen Army which he had helped to
form to defend the transport workers in the Dublin strike of 1913, was
more of a realist. He believed that a successful rebellion was possible
if it secured the support of the Irish masses. The revolutionaries also
hoped to obtain arms from Germany, and indeed Sir Roger

Casement, a former British diplomat and a fanatical supporter of the Irish cause, had gone from the United States to Germany in October 1914 (financed by Irish-American funds) to obtain German support for an Irish revolution.

Plans for the rebellion were organised by Clarke, MacDermott, Pearse and Connolly and their tiny band of fellow conspirators in conditions of intense secrecy, both for security reasons and because they were aware that MacNeill was against such action. Their plan was to begin the uprising in Dublin through the Volunteers, under the guise of ordinary field manoeuvres, and at a time when the city would be relatively deserted and the authorities off guard. Hence, on the morning of Easter Monday (24 April) 1916, a small detachment of Irish Volunteers and members of the Irish Citizen Army, headed by Pearse, Connolly and other leaders, marched into central Dublin – without a shot being fired – and seized control of the General Post Office. There they made their headquarters. Pearse then read out the famous proclamation announcing the birth of the Irish republic: 'We declare the right of the people of Ireland to the ownership of Ireland, and to the unfettered control of Irish destinies, to be sovereign and indefeasible … Standing on that fundamental right and again asserting it in arms in the face of the world, we hereby proclaim the Irish republic as a sovereign independent state.' A provisional government was established with himself as head.

By nightfall most of the key buildings in the city of Dublin were in the hands of the rebels. But as a serious military enterprise the Easter Rebellion was doomed from the start. The rebellion was mostly confined to Dublin, and most citizens there were bemused or downright hostile. Indeed many felt that the rebels were simply traitors, stabbing Britain in the back when so many Irishmen were fighting and dying in France. Strategically, the success of the rebellion depended on the participation of the provincial units of the Volunteers; but this did not take place. MacNeill got wind of Pearse's plans and used his authority as Chief of Staff to ban military activity by the Volunteers over the weekend, and the provincial units obeyed. Nor did the rebels receive any outside help. A German ship carrying arms to the rebels had been intercepted by the Royal Navy on 20 April, and on the following day Sir Roger Casement, who was landed on the coast of Ireland by a German submarine, was captured.

It is true that the British authorities, who had never taken the earlier activities of the Irish Volunteers very seriously, were caught unawares by the outbreak of the rebellion in Dublin. But even on Easter Monday the rebels were outnumbered by soldiers and armed police. When reinforcements and artillery were brought into action on the following day, the position of Pearse and his comrades, despite their fervour and bravery, was hopeless. British shelling set the General Post Office ablaze, and the rebel leaders were forced to flee and join their comrades in other parts of the city, where there was fierce fighting and much destruction of property. Then the rebels were hunted down, and within a week it was all over. On Saturday (29 April) Patrick Pearse, on behalf of the rebel forces, surrendered unconditionally to the British authorities. It has been estimated that about 450 rebels and civilians (mainly the latter) were killed during the rebellion and about 2,000 wounded. On the British side, 116 soldiers and police were killed and 3–400 wounded.

b) The Aftermath

The Easter Rebellion of 1916 was in no sense a national rising: only about 1,600 men and women participated on the rebel side, most of them supporters of one section of the Irish Volunteers (the National Volunteers remained loyal), and the rebellion was therefore made 'by a minority of a minority'. It was condemned by the Catholic Church, and denounced by Redmond and the moderate nationalists. Public opinion was generally hostile. Yet within a few weeks Irish attitudes towards the rebellion began to change. This was mainly due to the policies now adopted by the British authorities.

Characteristically, Asquith handed over the problem of dealing with the aftermath of the rebellion to the army. Martial law had been proclaimed in Dublin and then throughout Ireland at the beginning of Easter Week. As a result General Maxwell, the British Commander-in-Chief, applied a draconian policy of wholesale arrests, followed by imprisonment or internment and accompanied by a number of executions, in an attempt (it has been said) 'to destroy revolutionary nationalism root and branch'. About 3,000 Irish men and women

PROFILE: EAMON DE VALERA (1882–1975)

-Profile-

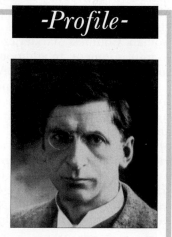

The (probably) illegitimate child, born in New York, to a Spanish father and Irish mother, de Valera was educated in Ireland and for a time taught mathematics there. He joined the Gaelic League, and later the Irish Volunteers, and fought in the Easter Rising, being the last commander to surrender. Only his American citizenship saved him from execution. After a short period of imprisonment, his reputation as the sole leading figure to survive the Rising helped him become leader of both Sinn Fein and the Irish Volunteers. In 1918, despite being imprisoned, he was elected an MP, and after breaking out of jail became President of the newly-formed Dail. His political ideal was a Gaelic republic comprising all 32 Irish counties.

For most of the Anglo-Irish war he was in the United States, raising money for the Irish cause. After the truce in July 1921 he held talks with Lloyd George (who commented that negotiating with him was 'like trying to pick up mercury with a fork'), but he controversially absented himself from the crucial talks held n London during October-December 1921. Perhaps he wanted his rival, Michael Collins, to receive the blame likely to attach to an unpopular settlement. It is, however, hard to judge the motives of such an ascetic, wily personality. Certainly he disapproved of the terms that were reached and led the anti-treaty forces in the civil war. Then he changed course, splitting with the militant Sinn Feiners in 1926 and forming his own party, the *Fianna Fail*. He was head of the Irish government in 1932–48, 1951–4 and 1957–9. He was President from 1959 until his death (aged 90) in 1957. W.B. Yeats once said that he was 'a living argument rather than a living man', but he was undoubtedly the most important Irish politician of the twentieth century.

were arrested; about half of these were soon released, but 160 suffered terms of imprisonment and most of the remainder were interned in England and Wales. 90 prisoners were tried and sentenced to death; and 15 of the condemned – including all seven signatories of the Easter Monday Proclamation – were executed early in May. James Connolly was unable to stand, so he was shot sitting in a chair. The remaining 75 – including Eamon de Valera and one woman, Countess Markievicz – had their death sentences commuted to imprisonment. In addition, Roger Casement was hanged for treason at Pentonville Prison in August 1916.

The harshness of these measures – and the callous way in which some of the executions were carried out, together with reports of ill-treatment of prisoners and intimidation of civilians – aroused horror and resentment amongst all classes in southern Ireland. (Bernard Shaw remarked that the British were 'canonising their prisoners'.) Hence the rebels were given moral credence, and Irish nationalists were able to ignore the fact that in some ways the Rising had been a fiasco. Anti-war and anti-British sentiments in Ireland were hardened, as John Dillon (Redmond's second-in-command) pointed out in an outstanding speech in the House of Commons on 11 May:

I The great bulk of the population were not favourable to the insurrection, and the insurgents themselves, who had confidently calculated on a rising of the people in their support, were absolutely disappointed. They got no popular support whatsoever. What is happening is that

5 thousands of people in Dublin, who ten days ago were bitterly opposed
to the whole of the Sinn Fein movement and to the rebellion, are now
becoming infuriated against the government on account of these executions, and, as I am informed by letters received this morning, that
feeling is spreading throughout the country in a most dangerous degree.

As a result of these reactions, as well as pressure from the United
States government, Asquith concluded that a new effort must be
made to secure an Irish settlement immediately, and Lloyd George
was put in charge of negotiations. Lloyd George proposed to both
Redmond and Carson a Home Rule solution based on the exclusion
of the six mainly Protestant counties of Ulster, and managed to get
both sides to accept it. But this was typical sleight of hand on his part,
for Redmond was led to believe that the exclusion was temporary,
while Carson thought that the exclusion of the six counties would be
permanent. Lloyd George's house of cards collapsed anyway, since
the key Unionists in the Coalition government were against any
immediate grant of Home Rule.

For Redmond the failure of the negotiations was a personal disaster. His apparent willingness to accept the partition of Ireland led to
his denunciation by important sections of Irish opinion, and his personal influence, and that of his party, declined ever more rapidly.
'Enthusiasm and trust in Redmond is dead', one Irish MP noted, 'so
far as the mass of the people is concerned'. Thus, as the historian
F.S.L. Lyons observes: 'the whole constitutional movement, in the last
analysis, was the chief casualty of 1916'. It was Sinn Fein – conspicu-
ous by its absence from the negotiations of that year – that now came
to occupy the place formerly held by Redmond's Parliamentary Party
as the dominant force in Irish nationalism.

3 Sinn Fein

> **KEY ISSUE** How is the growth of Sinn Fein, from rebel
> organisation to provisional government, best explained?

a) The Rise of Sinn Fein

Sinn Fein ('Ourselves Alone' or 'Our Own Thing') had been founded
by Arthur Griffith in 1907 as a militant, but non-violent, Irish nationalist organisation. It had had little influence before the war, and its anti-
war stance in 1914 remained a minority view. What changed the
situation was the Easter Rebellion of 1916. The cult of 'the men of
1916' as heroes and martyrs, which developed virtually from the
moment of their execution, and the growth of the historical myth –
cultivated both by their friends and their enemies – that the Easter
Rebellion was essentially a Sinn Fein uprising, increased the prestige

and influence of Griffith's organisation at the expense of the Irish Parliamentary Party. Sinn Fein's popularity increased even more as a result of the policies pursued by the British government and the army after May 1916: the continuation of martial law and further imprisonments, including that of Arthur Griffith himself; the creation of fresh martyrs owing to the deaths of a few prisoners on hunger strike; the spread of revolutionary ideas among the Irishmen brought together in the prisons and internment camps; and the apparent acceptance of the Unionist veto over immediate Home Rule by Asquith and Lloyd George. By the end of 1916 Sinn Fein had in effect remodelled itself to conform with its current image: it was a revolutionary party committed to the establishment of the Irish Republic whose birth had been announced in the Easter Monday Proclamation.

The changing trend of opinion in Ireland was seen when, early in 1917, Sinn Fein won two by-elections in usually safe Redmondite seats. In April the United States entered the war on the side of the Allies, and as a result of pressure from President Woodrow Wilson for an Irish settlement, Lloyd George (who had replaced Asquith as Prime Minister in December 1916) released the Irish prisoners held in internment in Great Britain. All this did was to provide new, more revolutionary, recruits for Sinn Fein. He then followed this up by summoning an Irish Convention in July 1917, representing the British government and all parties in Ireland, to try once again to hammer out an Irish settlement. The Convention scheme has been called 'a masterstroke of improvisation', since Lloyd George's real intention was to keep the Irishmen talking for as long as possible while he got on with the task of winning the war. In this he was successful in that the Convention staggered on until May 1918. But as far as an Irish settlement was concerned it was a complete failure, since Sinn Fein boycotted the Convention and the Ulster Unionists remained as immovable as ever. This drove another nail into the coffin of the Irish Parliamentary Party, as Redmond had pinned all his last hopes for immediate Home Rule on to the Convention. Its failure left him isolated and bereft of ideas. He died in May 1918, during the last days of the conference, a sad and disappointed man.

More significant than the summoning of the Irish Convention in July 1917 was the election that same month of Eamon de Valera as Sinn Fein MP for East Clare. His election was clearly 'a vote for 1916'. Sinn Fein now extended and strengthened its organisation. At its national conference in October 1917 de Valera was elected President in succession to Arthur Griffith, and in the following month he became head of the Irish Volunteers, thus combining in his person the leadership of both the political and military wings of the Irish revolutionary movement. By October 1917 too there were some 1,200 Sinn Fein clubs throughout Ireland, with a total of about 250,000 members. By 1918 (writes the Irish historian Roy Foster) Sinn Fein 'had succeeded to the position enjoyed by Parnell's Irish Parliamentary Party in the 1880s'. What strengthened its position even further was the conscription crisis that emerged in Ireland that same year.

b) The Conscription Crisis and the General Election of 1918

As a result of the heavy and continuous demand for manpower which followed the German spring offensive of 1918 on the western front, the British government began to contemplate the introduction of conscription in Ireland. There, owing to gathering opposition to 'England's War', the 1916 Conscription Act had not been applied. The necessary legislation was, nevertheless, pushed through parliament in May 1918. 'All Ireland will rise against you', John Dillon (who had succeeded Redmond as leader of the Irish Parliamentary Party) warned Lloyd George, and indeed (outside Ulster) that is exactly what happened. Dillon and his party displayed their opposition by walking out of the House of Commons and going to Dublin where, in alliance with Sinn Fein, they organised a nationwide campaign against conscription. A successful one-day strike was also mounted by the Irish trade unions, and the Roman Catholic Church in Ireland denounced conscription as oppressive and inhumane. The government then gave way before this barrage of opposition, so that in fact conscription was not made operative. But by this time damage had been done to the cause of the Union.

It was Sinn Fein which gained most from this radicalisation of opinion in southern Ireland, and its agitation was directed almost as much against the Irish Parliamentary Party as the British government. As Dillon said, presciently, Sinn Fein's purpose was 'to swallow us up', and indeed the alliance between the two organisations soon collapsed. The changing trend in Irish opinion was seen in microcosm when in April 1918 Arthur Griffith (now Vice-President of Sinn Fein) was returned for East Cavan against a constitutionalist candidate by an overwhelming majority. The authorities in Ireland responded to all this in typically obtuse fashion by arresting Republican leaders (with the excuse of their involvement in a 'German plot'), and clamping down on public meetings and the press. Yet this antagonised public opinion and played into Sinn Fein's hands. The results were seen in the general election held in December 1918, shortly after the signing of the November Armistice which ended the war. In Ireland the election proved to be a bitter and ugly affair. Its consequences, however, were decisive for the future of the country.

Sinn Fein fought the 1918 election on the basis of the principles enshrined in the Easter Monday Proclamation. This meant support for an independent, united Irish Republic, and the destruction – by 'any and every means available' – of English power over Ireland. Any Irish party demanding less than complete independence was to be opposed. The problem of Ulster was ignored: Ulster unionism was, affirmed de Valera, 'a thing of the mind only, non-existent in the world of reality'. The result of the 1918 general election was an overwhelming victory for Sinn Fein, and the virtual destruction of the Irish Parliamentary Party. Sinn Fein won 73 seats, the Parliamentary Party just six (compared with 68 in December 1910); the Unionists obtained 26. In terms of votes, however, in a much enlarged electorate (the result of the 1918 Reform Act), the results were slightly less impressive: 48 per cent of the votes were cast for Sinn Fein (though 25 of their candidates were returned unopposed); 31 per cent of electors did not vote; nor did the Irish Labour Party stand as a separate party. On the other hand, in the Twenty-Six counties of Catholic Ireland, Sinn Fein did win 65 per cent of the votes cast.

Sinn Fein could now realistically claim to represent the will of the Irish majority. The election had given it legitimacy. Its MPs decided, therefore, not to take their seats in the House of Commons, thus implicitly refusing to recognise the authority of the United Kingdom parliament over Ireland. Instead, Sinn Fein summoned all its MPs to Dublin on 21 January 1919, to constitute themselves as the Parliament of the Irish Republic (Dail Eireann). Only 27 arrived, but then the rest were either in prison or involved elsewhere. The Dail issued a Declaration of Independence, and demanded an English withdrawal from Ireland, and set up a Provisional government under de Valera. In March the British government, perplexed and bewildered by these recent events, released all the Irish political prisoners, thus strengthening Sinn Fein's hand. The Irish Provisional government was soon able to make its authority effective over much of Ireland, where it established its own courts of law and even collected taxes. It was backed up by the power of the Irish Republican Army (IRA), as the Irish Volunteers were now coming to be called, under its brilliant leader, Michael Collins. Collins, who had fought in Dublin during the Easter Rebellion of 1916, was both an outstanding military commander and a practical statesman. He was to organise the intelligence system that proved so vital to the IRA during the Anglo-Irish war of 1919–21, and he also held important domestic posts in the Irish Provisional government.

Thus by 1919 two authorities confronted one another in Ireland, both demanding the allegiance of the Irish people: the British government, which rested its mandate upon law and established treaty rights, and the Irish Provisional government, which claimed to represent the will of the Irish people and embody Irish nationhood. How would the deadlock be resolved? In January 1919 two policemen in County Tipperary had been killed by the IRA during an attempt to obtain explosives from a local quarry. For Sinn Fein and the IRA this marked the opening shots in what they regarded as a war for Irish independence. By that time, however, the British government was already planning a new constitutional initiative for the whole of Ireland.

4 The Government of Ireland Act, 1920

> **KEY ISSUES** Did the Act fail because it gave 'too little, too late'?

Outside Ireland, the result of the general election of December 1918 was an overwhelming victory for the Coalition government of Lloyd George, who was supported by the Conservatives (with nearly 400 MPs) and a section of the Liberals. The other part of the Liberal Party, led by Asquith, together with the Labour Party, were now in opposition. For the government the Irish question was bound to re-emerge as an important priority, not only because of Sinn Fein's recent victory in the Irish elections, but because the application of the 1914 Home Rule Act had only been postponed until the end of the war. The Irish question still begged a proper answer.

Yet the profound changes in British party politics since 1914, together with the new emphasis on national self-determination enshrined in the declarations of the peacemakers at Paris, were bound to affect the Irish question. Indeed, the Coalition government had announced in 1918 that one of its first tasks was to 'explore all practical paths towards a settlement of this grave and difficult question on the basis of self-government'. This consensus over self-government ('we are all Home Rulers now', as one Tory MP observed) meant that the Conservative Party – all apart from a few 'diehard' MPs – distanced itself from the Ulster Unionists and was no longer prepared in principle to oppose Home Rule, so long as it could be coupled with a recognition of Ulster's rights and the retention of Ireland within the Empire.

Nevertheless Ulster Unionists were still in a relatively strong position. A number of them were in the government, and Carson (who had been returned for a Belfast constituency in 1918) was still an influential figure outside. In the House of Commons the Conservative Party was dominant; and the Ulster Unionists (who had won 22 out of 37 seats in Northern Ireland) formed the only distinct Irish voice at Westminster, since the Sinn Fein MPs refused to take their seats. Moreover, Lloyd George – who remembered his disastrous experience over the Irish negotiations in 1916 – was determined this time to ensure that any proposed Irish settlement received the backing of his Conservative colleagues. Walter Long (a former leader of the Ulster Unionists) was appointed chairman of the government's Irish Committee with the task of producing a new Home Rule bill.

The main feature of the eventual government plan for Ireland was the application of the principle of Home Rule to both Ulster and southern Ireland. The Government of Ireland Bill of 1920 therefore proposed the establishment of two separate parliaments for Northern and Southern Ireland, consisting of an elected House of Commons and a Senate (Upper House), together with a government responsible to each parliament. In order to safeguard the rights of minorities in each region, election to the two parliaments was to be by proportional representation. The powers of the parliaments were to be similar to those contained in the 1914 Home Rule Act, which meant that though they were responsible for most internal affairs, the Imperial government would still retain considerable control. Thus, the new parliaments were to have no jurisdiction over foreign policy, defence, external trade, customs, police or even the Post Office. It was also written into the Act that the supremacy of the United Kingdom Parliament remained 'unaffected and undiminished over all persons, matters and things in Ireland', in order to justify the British government's intervention in the affairs of Northern Ireland.

As far as the vexed question of the boundaries of Northern Ireland was concerned, the Coalition government eventually accepted the Ulster Unionist argument in favour of six counties (see page 122) on the grounds that, owing to their overall Protestant majority, security and stability in the new state would be made easier. Both parts of Ireland were to be represented at Westminster. There was also to be a Council of Ireland, consisting of representatives from both North and South, to deal with common problems; and it was written into the Act that, if both sides consented, one common parliament could be established for the whole country. For Lloyd George, this represented one final appeal to the old Liberal Party ideal of Home Rule for the whole of Ireland.

The Ulster Unionists, who had not originally wanted self-government within the United Kingdom, eventually came to see the advantages of the new proposals, particularly in the light of the IRA's violent campaign throughout Ireland (described in the next section). 'We see our safety in having a Parliament of our own,' wrote Captain Charles Craig (brother of the Ulster Unionist leader); 'we feel that we would then be in a position of absolute security'. The Government of Ireland Bill therefore easily passed through parliament at the end of 1920, and its terms came into operation in May 1921. In the elections for the Northern Ireland parliament that shortly followed, the Unionists won 40 out of the 52 seats, and as a result Sir James Craig became Prime Minister and began the formidable task of taking over powers from the British authorities and providing peace and stability in the new state.

In the south, however, the Act was virtually a dead letter. No elections were contested, and 124 supporters of Sinn Fein (which by that time was still fighting a war against England) were returned unopposed out of 128 candidates. To show their contempt for the Act, the Sinn Feiners then boycotted the new parliament as they had already done with the Westminster parliament after the elections of 1918. Thus, paradoxically, it was the Ulster Unionists who were now the committed Home Rulers. In Southern Ireland, on the other hand, the political revolution which had been gathering pace since 1916 had left Home Rule far behind as a viable option for Irish nationalists. The Government of Ireland Act, therefore, as Roy Foster suggests, was 'essentially constructed to solve the Irish problem as it stood in 1914 not in 1920'.

5 The Anglo-Irish War, 1919–21

> **KEY ISSUE** Why did the Anglo-Irish conflict become so bloody and unrestrained?

At the same time as the British government was introducing the Government of Ireland Act, it was also trying to cope with the activities of the IRA throughout much of Ireland. From the beginning of 1919 the IRA, under the leadership of Michael Collins, had launched a campaign of murder and harassment directed mainly against the police, and British soldiers, in an effort to destroy English power in Ireland and force England to withdraw. For Sinn Fein and the IRA, their campaign was a legitimate one on behalf of an existing Irish Republic, and they expected to be treated as the soldiers of an Irish national army. *The Volunteer's Journal* (31 January 1919) put their position clearly.

1 If they are called on to shed their blood in defence of the new-born Republic they will not shrink from the sacrifice. For the authority of the nation is behind them, embodied in a lawfully constituted authority ... Dail Eireann, in its message to the Free Nations of the World, declares
5 a 'state of war' to exist between Ireland and England ... [which] can never be ended until the English military invader evacuates our country ... The 'state of war' which is thus declared to exist ... justifies Irish Volunteers in treating the armed forces of the enemy – whether soldiers or policemen – exactly as a National Army would treat the mem-
10 bers of an invading army ... Every Volunteer is entitled, morally and legally in the execution of his military duties, to use all legitimate methods of warfare against the soldiers and policemen of the English usurper, and to slay them if it is necessary to do so in order to overcome their resistance.

The British government found it difficult to know how to respond to these tactics. In their eyes the IRA were just members of a tiny 'murder gang' (in Lloyd George's description), unrepresentative of and alien to the mass of the Irish people. They were not and should not be treated as genuine combatants. But the government had no clear, positive policy to offer, and little understanding of what was really happening on the ground in Ireland. It was subject to the pulls and pressures of the military authorities on the spot and public opinion in Britain. For a long time Lloyd George and the Cabinet refused to recognise the existence of a state of war in Ireland, or the alienation of the Catholic masses from British rule and their sympathy with Sinn Fein's demand for independence. Lloyd George, under pressure from his Conservative backbenchers and busy with other problems, therefore reverted to the time-honoured expedient of repression. Sinn Fein and the IRA became proscribed organisations; the Dail was declared illegal; special powers of arrest, imprisonment and arms control were introduced; and attempts were made to ban revolutionary publications.

To maintain law and order the authorities relied at first primarily on the police. But the Royal Irish Constabulary (RIC) were undermanned and much demoralised by the IRA's murder campaign directed mainly against them: 176 policemen were killed in 1920, compared with 54 soldiers. The police were therefore strengthened by the recruitment of tough, ex-soldiers, who became known as the 'Black-and-Tans' (since they wore khaki uniforms with the black belts and peaked caps of the RIC). Later, the Auxiliaries ('Auxis') were formed, consisting of ex-army officers who acted as an ill-disciplined, semi-military force.

During 1920 the IRA campaign became more widespread, more calculated and more brutal. It was now directed against civilians who could be regarded as giving comfort to 'the enemy', as well as the police and soldiers, and was accompanied by attacks on public buildings and isolated atrocities. The Black-and-Tans responded in kind, and their unofficial reprisals were in effect condoned by the British army and the government. This attitude did not go uncondemned in Great Britain, especially by the press. Even the Conservative *Daily Express* proclaimed 'murder for murder is ... a confession of impotence, a return to sheer barbarism'. In fact, the politicians had little control over the forces on either side.

In the autumn of 1920 the British government at last accepted that it was engaged in real war in Ireland, and it now applied regular troops on a wider scale and introduced martial law in the south. Neither side, however, paid much attention to the ordinary laws of war. This last phase of the Anglo-Irish conflict became a grim affair of terror and counter-terror, ambush and atrocities, and the intimidation and occasional murder of civilians. One of the worst episodes of the whole war – but symptomatic of the nature of the conflict – took place on 'Bloody Sunday', 21 November 1920, in Dublin. In the morning 11 English civilians (believed to be working for British Intelligence) were shot dead by the IRA in the homes and hotels where they were staying. The Black-and-Tans had their revenge in the afternoon. They invaded the sports ground of Croke Park and fired indiscriminately at the players and the crowd, leaving behind 12 dead and 60 wounded. In December much of Cork was burnt, as a reprisal for the killing of 'Auxis' in two ambushed lorries.

By early 1921, however, it was clear that militarily the Anglo-Irish war was winnable by neither side. The IRA (as Collins accepted) was incapable of defeating the British army, and they were getting short of men and materials as casualties among their members and civilians became heavier. Between 1 January and July 1921 it is estimated that 752 men and women (IRA and civilians) were killed and 866 wounded. Equally, however, the British government was not prepared to use its full power in an all-out war against Catholic Ireland, which is what real victory would have entailed. Once these basic facts were recognised there was the possibility of a truce and negotiations between the two sides.

6 The Anglo-Irish Treaty, 1921

> **KEY ISSUES** Why was the Treaty accepted by Sinn Fein representatives? Should it be seen as a success or a failure?

a) The Truce

By the end of 1920 Lloyd George was profoundly aware of the growing unpopularity of the Anglo-Irish war in Great Britain and anxious to find a way out. There was a deep revulsion against the methods pursued by the Black-and-Tans especially, which was expressed by church leaders, opposition spokesmen – 'a state of affairs prevails which is a disgrace to the human race', said Labour's Arthur Henderson – the trade union movement, and, above all, influential newspapers such as *The Times* and the *Manchester Guardian*. Opinion in the United States had also been shocked.

The Prime Minister was informed by his military advisers that it would require an army of 100,000 to subjugate Ireland, and it was obvious that public opinion would never stand for such an operation. Hence, as George Boyce writes: 'it was the revolt of the British conscience, not the defeat of the British army, that obliged Lloyd George to seek terms of peace and settlement with Sinn Fein'. Moreover, the Prime Minister had at last come to realise that he was faced not just with opposition from a tiny 'murder gang', but with a formidable movement whose demands for independence were backed up by the majority of the Irish people.

In December 1920 Lloyd George put out peace feelers to de Valera in an effort to bring about a truce and negotiations, but these early moves failed. Nevertheless, the fact that a British Prime Minister was prepared to consider such a step represented a breakthrough in Anglo-Irish relations and (it has been suggested) a psychological victory for Sinn Fein. Lloyd George's determination to persist with his peace efforts was reinforced by reactions to the implementation of the Government of Ireland Act in the spring of 1921. The blunt refusal of Sinn Fein to have anything to do with the Southern Ireland parliament set up under the Act, not only showed its determination to consider nothing less than effective independence, but also raised the question: how were the Twenty-Six counties to be governed now if Home Rule was ruled out? The alternatives seemed to be either all-out war and military rule, or peace and negotiations, and the first option was in practice impossible. The fact that a separate (six-county) Northern Ireland state was now a *fait accompli* helped to remove an additional complication to any truce and future negotiations. In that sense (as one historian suggests), 'Partition cleared the way for the treaty [of 1921]'.

Peace in fact came quite suddenly. The catalyst is generally considered to have been the words of King George V in a speech given at the opening of the Northern Ireland parliament in Belfast on 22 June 1921.

> I appeal to all Irishmen to pause, to stretch out the hand of forbearance and conciliation, to forgive and forget and to join in making for the land which they love a new era of peace, contentment and good will.

Yet in fact these words cut little ice with the Irish Republicans, given the fact that they emanated from the very citadel of Ulster separatism. What moved de Valera and Collins more were hard military facts: the loss of men and weapons and the exhaustion produced by the war. They could only have carried on for another three weeks, Collins said later. The Republican leaders also came to accept that Lloyd George was genuinely seeking a political settlement and was prepared to moderate his original conditions for peace in order to obtain one. The Prime Minister was in fact already thinking in terms of 'Dominion Status' as the basis for such a settlement. Both sides therefore agreed to a truce on 11 July 1921.

b) The Treaty

The truce was followed almost immediately by meetings between Lloyd George and de Valera, as well as Sir James Craig, which formed the prelude to a long period of complicated negotiations which lasted almost until the end of the year. The basis of Lloyd George's proposal for a political settlement was the offer of Dominion Status, that is, granting to Ireland the same constitutional powers as belonged to Canada and other Dominions within the British Empire. This was a considerable advance on Home Rule, though it was less than complete independence. Dominion Status for Ireland meant full control of domestic affairs but also membership of the British Empire and allegiance to the Crown. In addition, the Prime Minister insisted on naval facilities in Ireland, and recognition of the state of Northern Ireland 'which cannot be abrogated except by their own consent'.

The British government's original proposals were rejected out of hand by the hard-line Republican majority in the Dail Eireann (Irish parliament), for whom the oath of allegiance and membership of the British Empire were too much to stomach. De Valera himself, however, was prepared to accept some sort of connection with Great Britain. What was needed, therefore, was a form of words – and much of the discussion in the long months ahead turned on such verbal niceties – which would reconcile the reality of Irish independence with formal membership of the Empire. De Valera agreed to send a delegation to London on 11 October 1921, to negotiate with the British representatives 'with a view to ascertain how the association of Ireland with the community of nations known as the British empire may best be reconciled with Irish national aspirations'.

The five-man Irish delegation which assembled in London in October was led by Arthur Griffith and Michael Collins. De Valera preferred to remain in Dublin as the symbol of 'the Republic', unsullied by the processes of bargaining taking place in London. This produced tension between the Irish leaders in Dublin and their colleagues in London, a situation which was worsened by the confusion over the status of the Irish delegates. On the one hand, they were described as plenipotentiaries, and could therefore sign a binding treaty with the British government on their own authority; on the other hand, de Valera insisted that any draft treaty arrived at be submitted first to the government back home. These misunderstandings among the Irish leaders gave a considerable advantage to the British team, and especially to a man as experienced and skilled in negotiation as Lloyd George. For it was the Prime Minister who really dominated the London conference. He had three government ministers as his colleagues, Winston Churchill, Austen Chamberlain (leader of the Conservative Party) and Lord Birkenhead. But the last two were there primarily to ensure that Lloyd George received the backing of the Conservative Party for any Irish settlement that he was able to secure.

There were three main questions for discussion by the two groups of delegates: 1) the powers of the new Irish state, 2) Ulster, 3) British security and defence. The last question was, remarkably, settled fairly easily when it was agreed that Great Britain should have three naval bases in Ireland. Even the question of Ulster did not prove in the end as difficult as might have been expected. None of the Irish leaders in London or Dublin wanted partition but none was really prepared to challenge the existence of the new state of Northern Ireland. Though the proposed treaty was to apply to the whole of Ireland, Northern

Ireland was therefore given the right to opt out. In addition, Lloyd George persuaded the Irish delegates to accept the idea of a Boundary Commission, and led them to believe that its eventual recommendations would be so critical of Ulster's present boundaries that, if carried out, the Northern Ireland state would collapse and have to join up with the rest of Ireland. The Prime Minister also agreed to bring Northern Ireland into line over this proposal, but this was pure bluff, since there was no way in which Sir James Craig could be coerced into agreeing to co-operate with any such scheme, and in fact later negotiations to alter the boundary between the two states got nowhere.

Nevertheless, the offer of the Boundary Commission did help to resolve what proved to be the most contentious issue at the conference: the old problem of Ireland's relationship to the Crown and the Empire. Characteristically, for both sides this was more an argument about symbols than political realities. In the end, however, partly in return for the offer of the Boundary Commission, Lloyd George managed to get the Irish delegates to accept a cosmetic formula over the Crown and Empire issues. Southern Ireland would have Dominion Status rather than the independence Sinn Fein wanted, but the oath of allegiance to the Crown would be watered down, making it less offensive to Irish sensibilities. After much to-ing and fro-ing between London and Dublin – where there was considerable opposition to the proposed treaty – matters were brought to a head.

On the afternoon of Monday 5 December the Prime Minister laid down a threat. Unless the Sinn Fein representatives accepted the treaty 'it is war, and war within three days ... We must have your answer by ten p.m. tonight. You can have until then, but no longer, to decide whether you will give peace or war to your country.' Mesmerised by Lloyd George, fearful of the consequences of rejection and worn out by months of negotiation, Griffith, Collins and their three colleagues reluctantly agreed to sign the Anglo-Irish Treaty – at 2.30 a.m. on 6 December 1921. Collins insisted, quite rightly, that he was signing his own death warrant. Yet the irony is that Lloyd George may have been bluffing with his threat to resume the war. Certainly British public opinion would have been profoundly against a resumption the Anglo-Irish war (which had already tarnished Britain's reputation in the world).

c) The Results of the Treaty

In Great Britain the treaty was clearly popular with the public, and, despite the misgivings of many Conservatives, the signatures of their party leaders, Chamberlain and Birkenhead, on the document, ensured that it passed comfortably through parliament on 16 December 1921. In Ireland, on the other hand, the reception of the treaty was very different: there it brought not unity but discord and conflict. The Irish Cabinet was divided over whether the treaty should be accepted or rejected. Collins believed that there was no possibility of getting better terms from Lloyd George, and no alternative to acceptance but renewed and fiercer warfare. De Valera, who was opposed to the treaty since it included the oath of loyalty to the King, resigned as President and was succeeded by Griffith. The Dail, however, after a series of passionate debates, supported the treaty by the narrow majority of 64 votes to 57 on 7 January 1922, and, as in Britain, public opinion was generally in favour.

The terms of the Anglo-Irish Treaty were carried out almost immediately. A new Provisional Government was appointed under Michael Collins, and power was formally handed over to it by the British Viceroy on 16 January. The British army then began the process of withdrawing from Ireland, and handing over its barracks and facilities to the IRA. In June 1922 a general election was held in Ireland which gave Collins and the pro-Treaty group a convincing majority. The anti-Treaty faction, however, led by de Valera, refused to accept the verdict, and 'the Troubles' – a civil war in Ireland more brutal and more destructive than the earlier Anglo-Irish war – followed. When the violence spread to Northern Ireland, many Conservatives regretted supporting the scheme, a major factor in Lloyd George's fall in October 1922. In the spring of 1923, however, the rebels made their peace with the new regime.

By the end of 1922 the Irish government (now headed by William Cosgrove, following the death of Arthur Griffith and the murder of Collins by rebels) felt it was strong enough to promulgate a formal Constitution for the Irish Free State. It was approved by the Irish Dail in December and accepted by the British government. It was followed immediately by the government of Northern Ireland exercising its treaty right to opt out of the jurisdiction of the Irish Free State. By 1923, therefore, partition had triumphed. Two states existed side by side in the territory of Ireland: the Irish Free State and Northern Ireland.

The Anglo-Irish Treaty of 1921 was in many ways a flawed document, full of ambiguities and unresolved problems. The constitutional settlement was the product of no definite plan; it rested upon no clear-cut principles; it did not conform to the original ideals, or the deepest instincts, of any of the participants. As we saw earlier, the Ulster unionists had never wanted a separate state of their own, while for the Irish nationalist leaders the 1921 Treaty was a compromise which violated their commitment to a united Republican Ireland. The settlement also appeared to undermine the traditional views on Ireland of both Liberals and Conservatives, whose thinking had never gone beyond either support for or opposition to Home Rule. For the Coalition government too, as the Irish historian J.C. Beckett has observed, 'it was a solution that they adopted rather than created', and they adopted it for one overwhelming reason – because they believed that it would finally get rid of 'the Irish question'.

Yet the 1921 Treaty was by any reckoning an outstanding achievement. It brought the Anglo-Irish war to an end. It did more. 'It inaugurated for Ireland', says Beckett (writing in 1965), 'a longer period of general tranquillity than she had known since the first half of the eighteenth century'. In addition, Ireland now obtained a greater degree of independence than had been envisaged by O'Connell, or Parnell or Redmond. The Irish Free State completely controlled its own internal affairs – administration, education, justice, police and army, customs and taxes – and there were no Irish MPs at Westminster. Moreover the Anglo-Irish Treaty (together with the Government of Ireland Act of 1920) offered the possibility of eventual, peaceful, Irish unity. In return Great Britain obtained important provisions for her security.

All that remained of the Act of Union of 1801 was the largely symbolic office of Governor-General (the king's representative, which corresponded to the old office of Viceroy) and the purely verbal trappings of the oath of allegiance and membership of the British Empire. As Frank Pakenham (Lord Longford), author of the standard work on the 1921 Treaty, *Peace by Ordeal*, writes: 'Its deeper consequences transformed the whole system under which Ireland had previously been governed and the whole basis of Ireland's relationship to England. The British supremacy over Ireland first claimed in 1172 was virtually ended'.

The practical implications of this were seen in the following decades. One by one the provisions of the Treaty of 1921 which limited the sovereignty of the Irish Free State were rejected after 1932 by the Irish Prime Minister, Eamon de Valera, and accepted – more in sorrow than in anger – by Great Britain. In 1949, following the successful assertion of her neutrality during the Second World War, Eire (as the Free State was now called) cut the last remaining ties with Great Britain and the Commonwealth and became a fully independent Republic. Clement Attlee, the Labour Prime Minister, accepted Eire's new status, but insisted on passing the Ireland Act that same year. This affirmed the existing constitutional and territorial position of Northern Ireland, and insisted that no change could take place without 'the consent of the people of Northern Ireland' – a commitment that has governed British policy ever since. This commitment was to be of enormous importance when, just 20 years later, the Irish question re-emerged in an even more virulent fashion, this time in Ulster.

This was mainly the result of the character of the state of Northern Ireland created by the Government of Ireland Act of 1920. For Sir James Craig and the other Unionist leaders who came into power there after the general election of May 1921 – aware of the hostility of the large Catholic minority to the existence of the new state – proceeded to establish a regime based on Protestant domination. Politically, the power of the Protestant majority was underpinned by the abolition of proportional representation in local and parliamentary elections (as imposed by the 1920 Act), and the use of 'gerrymandering', by which the boundaries of local government areas and parliamentary constituencies were fixed, and re-fixed, so as to favour Protestant voters. In addition, special legislation gave the government extra-legal powers of arrest and imprisonment without trial in order to combat subversive activities, and the use of armed police – the Royal Ulster Constabulary and the notorious 'B' Special reserves – became part of the normal fabric of the state. 'We are', proclaimed Sir James Craig, 'a Protestant parliament and a Protestant state'. Nor was that domination confined to politics. Social and economic discrimination was practised openly against Catholics, particularly in the fields of housing and employment.

Successive British governments either ignored or tolerated the blatantly undemocratic and discriminatory policies pursued by the Ulster Unionist regime in Northern Ireland. Indeed (as we saw earlier) even a Labour government was prepared, implicitly, to support the status quo.

It was not until the end of the 1960s that a large-scale movement of opposition and agitation developed to remedy Catholic grievances, organised by the Civil Rights movement, generally in defiance of the authorities. This was followed by the outbreak of sectarian violence, the re-emergence of the IRA as the defenders of the Catholic communities in Belfast and Londonderry, and the gradual breakdown of law and order. In the summer of 1969 the British army was called in to maintain peace. 'Britain is once again up to its neck in the Irish Question', wrote *The Economist*. In 1968–70, 39 people were killed in Northern Ireland. Soon, mainly due to British pressure, some of the more obvious grievances of the Catholics had been remedied; but the evident inability of the Unionist government to cope with the violence in the province, or to win the trust of the minority community, led the British government to suspend the operation of the Stormont Parliament – as it had the right to do under the 1920 Act. Northern Ireland was again governed by direct rule from Westminster. Yet in 1972 around 450 died, and that year saw another 'Bloody Sunday' as 13 members of a civil rights march were killed by troops. Despite recent hopeful events, Northern Ireland is still the troublespot of the United Kingdom.

7 Conclusion

> **KEY ISSUE** How should the 1921 Anglo-Irish Treaty be seen in historical perspective?

The Act of Union of 1800, by swallowing up Ireland into the United

Kingdom, was in a way the logical outcome of the military conquest of that island in earlier centuries. The Act was undoubtedly conceived in terms of English and Protestant interests, from the point of view of security and defence, property rights and religion. Yet English politicians in the first half of the nineteenth century insisted that Ireland herself gained much from the Union. This was the result of British economic progress and the opportunities opened up for Irish Catholics after the Emancipation Act of 1829, as well as the 'modernisation' of Ireland pursued by successive British governments. Maintenance of the Union therefore became the bedrock of British policy for almost the next hundred years.

Nevertheless, once it became clear that the Irish majority were unprepared to accept membership of the United Kingdom on these terms, English politicians were faced with the grim reality of 'the Irish question'. This implied a recognition of the fact that Ireland was different from the rest of the United Kingdom and required special treatment. Hence the regimen of reform plus coercion which was carried out by successive British governments. This programme raised searching questions, however, about the relationship of Ireland to the rest of the UK. Why should time, effort and money be spent on Irish questions which were of no great concern to the majority of the British people? And how could a pro-Catholic policy of reform be reconciled with the needs of the Protestant minority in Ireland and the intense Protestantism of the British people? In addition, how could a liberal, and increasingly democratic, state justify the application to Ireland alone of special legislation outside the ordinary code of law? The conclusion drawn by many Victorian politicians was that the Irish question was (in the words of one of them) 'a troublesome and alien irruption into the British body politic'.

Compared with the earlier Victorian period, therefore, the main aim of British statesmen after 1885 was, in one way or another, to get rid of the Irish question in order to return to 'normal' British politics. The policy of Home Rule may be conceived as a means towards that end. However, by the time that Home Rule did become a practicable policy – after the passage of the 1911 Parliament Act – its Liberal protagonists were faced with the obstinate, unified opposition of the Ulster unionists until the end of the First World War. By the end of the war, as a result of the rise of Sinn Fein, Home Rule was in effect dead as an overall solution to the Irish question.

A more advanced alternative to Home Rule for Ireland was 'Dominion Status'. This meant virtually complete independence as far as domestic policy was concerned. It was this solution that was eventually applied by Lloyd George in the Anglo-Irish Treaty of 1921. Unfortunately, it was a solution that rested upon the partition of Ireland. It therefore came up against the powerful current of Irish Republican nationalism which had been given a new lease of life as a result of the Easter Rebellion of 1916. In its turn, however,

Republican nationalism was faced by the equally intransigent force of Ulster Protestantism based, after 1920, on its own state of Northern Ireland. The consequences of that confrontation – the outcome of nearly four centuries of Anglo-Irish history – remain with us today.

Summary Diagram

The Making of the Anglo-Irish Settlement of 1920–2

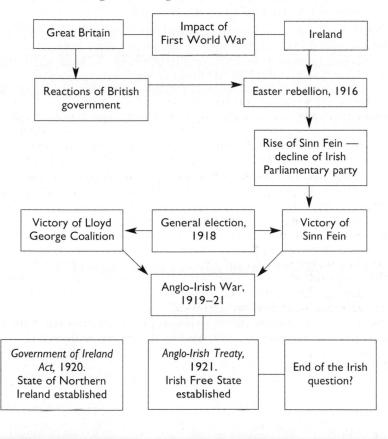

Working on Chapter 8

The years 1914–22 form a complex, dramatic and controversial period in Anglo-Irish history. Since your main concern is with the Irish question, your notes should concentrate on explaining British policy towards Ireland during this period. Bring in enough of the Irish background to enable you to do this effectively. Make detailed notes on the Anglo-Irish Treaty of 1921, and cover its results more briefly.

Answering structured and essay questions on Chapter 8

Two types of examination question are often asked on this period: (1) short-term questions dealing with specific issues, and, rather more often, (2) long-term questions covering the whole period. An example of the first type of question is:

1 'It changed the whole basis of Ireland's relationship to England.' Discuss this verdict on the Anglo-Irish Treaty of 1921.

Think how this somewhat uncomfortably large question might be broken down into smaller, more manageable ones (as perhaps in a structured question). Perhaps you might have: a) How was Ireland governed before 1921? b) What were the main provisions of the Treaty? c) How were Southern and Northern Ireland governed after 1922?

Typical of the second, longer-term question is:

2 Why did it prove so difficult to find a solution to the Irish question during the period 1912–22?

It is also worth considering a question which asks how effectively governed Ireland was in 1914–22. In order to test your understanding of this whole book, you might then change the dates to cover other periods from 1800 onwards.

Source-based questions on Chapter 8

1 The Anglo-Irish War, 1919–21

Read the extracts from Dillon's speech on page 132–3 and from the *Volunteer's Journal* on page 139. Answer the following questions.

a) What were the 'executions' referred to by Dillon? (*3 marks*)
b) Explain the reference in the second extract to 'the new-born Republic'. (*5 marks*)
c) Why was Dail Eireann claimed to be 'a lawfully constituted authority'? Why did the British government oppose this claim? (*6 marks*)
d) Why did the IRA insist on its status as a 'National Army'? (*5 marks*)
e) In what ways did both sides disregard 'legitimate methods of warfare'? (*6 marks*)
e) What factors other than those referred to by Dillon produced the state of affairs described in the *Volunteer's Journal*? (*10 marks*)

Further Reading

There are relatively few books that deal directly with Anglo-Irish relations, and therefore – since most readers will be familiar with the history of Britain – the best approach is to consider the topic through books on Irish history

1 General Surveys

The best introductory books on the subject are: **J.C. Beckett**, *The Making of Modern Ireland 1603–1923* (1969) and the multi-author volume, *The Course of Irish History* (1984 edn.) edited by T.W. Moody and F.X. Martin. Both provide lucid, narrative accounts. More advanced are: **F.S.L. Lyons**, *Ireland since the Famine* (1973) and **Roy Foster**, *Modern Ireland 1600–1922* (1989). Lyons' book is probably the more useful existing account for the student, while Foster's is a superlative 'revisionist' study, which (as we saw in the first chapter) has aroused enormous controversy among Irish historians. *The Oxford Companion to Irish History* (1998), edited by S.J. Connolly, is a mine of useful information.

There are also a number of other analytical surveys of modern Irish history. Among the most stimulating are: **K.T. Hoppen**, *Ireland since 1800: Conflict and Conformity* (1989); **Robert Kee**, *Ireland: A History* (1982), which is wonderfully illustrated; **George Boyce**, *Nineteenth-Century Ireland: the Search for Stability* (1990); **Oliver MacDonagh**, *Ireland: the Union and its Aftermath* (1977); and **John A. Murphy**, *Ireland in the Twentieth Century* (1975). **Alvin Jackson**, *Ireland 1798–1998* (1999) is very useful and very readable. **D.W. Harkness**, *Ireland in the Twentieth Century* (1995) is excellent.

2 Anglo-Irish Relations, 1800–1922

The following list is very much a 'mixed bag' of books expressing very different points of view on the subject. **George Boyce**, *The Irish Question and British Politics, 1868–1986* (1989), a helpful outline. **Roy Foster**, *Paddy and Mr. Punch: Connections in Irish and English History* (1993) covers a wide range of subjects and contains Foster's important article on 'History and the Irish Question'. **Hugh Kearney**, *The British Isles: A History of Four Nations* (1989), an almost unique attempt to consider together English, Irish, Welsh and Scottish history. **Oliver MacDonagh**, *States of Mind: A Study of Anglo-Irish Conflict 1780–1980* (1980), a penetrating analysis. **Nicholas Mansergh**, *The Irish Question 1840–1921* (1965), a wide-ranging study. **Patrick O'Farrell**, *England and Ireland since 1800* (1985), a concise account.

Specialist Studies

3 The Early Nineteenth Century

There are two excellent general accounts covering this period in Irish history: **E.M. Johnston**, *Ireland in the Eighteenth Century* (1972) and **G.O. Tuathaigh**, *Ireland before the Famine 1798–1848* (1972). On the British side there are: **I.R. Christie**, *Wars and Revolutions: Britain 1760–1815* (1982) and **Norman Gash**, *Aristocracy and People 1815–65* (1980). On Daniel O'Connell the major modern biography is by **Oliver MacDonagh** (2 vols, 1988 and 1989). Though a formidable work this can be dipped into with profit. An excellent short account is: **Fergus O'Ferrall**, *Daniel O'Connell* (1981). There are two important studies of O'Connell's politics: **Angus Macintyre**, *The Liberator: Daniel O'Connell and the Irish Party 1830–1847* (1965), and **Kevin B. Nowlan**, *The Politics of Repeal* (1965).

4 The Great Famine

There are two accessible accounts which are worth reading together. **Cecil Woodham-Smith**, *The Great Hunger* (1962), and **Mary E. Daly**, *The Famine in Ireland* (1986). Daly's is a short, academic study, Woodham-Smith's is a larger, more popular work. There is a short overview of the controversies surrounding the whole subject in **Cormac O'Grada**, *The Great Irish Famine* (1989). Also well worth consulting are the works of **Christine Kinealy**, including *The Great Calamity: the Irish Famine 1845–52* (1995) and *A Death-Dealing Famine: The Great Hunger in Ireland* (1997).

5 Gladstone and Ireland

On the Irish land question, the most useful account is the Lancaster Pamphlet by **M.J. Winstanley**, *Ireland and the Land Question* (1984). There is an important but difficult 'revisionist' study by **Barbara Solow**, *The Land Question and the Irish Economy 1870–1903* (Harvard University Press, 1971). A good overall view of Gladstone's political career is **E.J. Feuchtwanger**, *Gladstone* (1989); other excellent studies have been written by **H.C.G. Matthew**, **Richard Shannon** and **Roy Jenkins**. A classic, strongly favourable, study of his Irish policy is **J.L. Hammond**, *Gladstone and the Irish Nation* (1938). **A.B. Cooke** and **John Vincent** are more critical of Gladstone in *The Governing Passion: Cabinet Government and Party Politics in Britain 1885–6* (1974). There is an important book strongly critical of the Cooke/Vincent thesis: **J. Loughlin**, *Gladstone, Home Rule and the Ulster Question 1882–93* (1986).

6 Parnell and Irish Nationalism

On Parnell there are two outstanding modern biographies: **F.S.L. Lyons**, *Charles Stewart Parnell* (1977) and **Robert Kee**, *The Laurel and the Ivy: Parnell and Irish Nationalism* (1994). There is a short, penetrating study by **Paul Bew**, *Parnell* (1980). An interesting group of recent essays on the Irish leader is contained in **D.G. Boyce** and **Alan O'Day** (eds), *Parnell in Perspective* (1991). On Irish nationalism generally, see: **George Boyce**, *Nationalism in Ireland* (1982), the more popular account by **Robert Kee**, *The Green Flag* (1972), and **Alan O'Day**, *Irish Nationalism, 1798–1922* (1997).

7 Home Rule and Ulster Unionism, 1910–14

The outstanding study on the Irish question during this period is **Patricia Jalland**, *The Liberals and Ireland: The Ulster Question in British Politics to 1914* (1980). Easily the best introduction to Ulster unionism is the pamphlet by **Patrick Buckland**, *Irish Unionism* (1973). This is based on the same author's standard work, *Ulster Unionism and the Origins of Northern Ireland 1886–1922* (1973). Two books by **A.T.Q. Stewart** are especially helpful on the same subject: *Edward Carson* (1981), a short biography, and *The Ulster Crisis: Resistance to Home Rule, 1912–14* (1967), a detailed, narrative account. **Alvin Jackson's** *Sir Edward Carson* (1993) provides a biographical perspective.

8 The First World War and After, 1914–22

There are two very useful collections of short essays – many of them biographical – covering the whole period. **Desmond Williams** (ed), *The Irish Struggle 1916–1926* (1966) and **F.X. Martin** (ed), *Leaders and Men of the Easter Rising* (1967). The most helpful book on the political settlement of 1920–22 is **Michael Laffan**, *The Partition of Ireland 1911–1925* (1983). The standard account of the negotiations leading up to the 1921 Treaty is **Frank Pakenham** (Lord Longford), *Peace by Ordeal* (1935). All the standard biographies of Lloyd George comment on his involvement in Ireland. There is an interesting essay by **George Boyce** 'Lloyd George and Ireland' in *Lloyd George: Twelve Essays*, edited by A.J.P. Taylor (1971). Vital for the Anglo-Irish War is **Charles Townsend**, *The British Campaign in Ireland, 1919–21* (1975). On the nationalist side, **Michael Laffin's** *The Resurrection of Ireland: the Sinn Fein Party, 1916–23* (1999) is excellent. Biographies are provided by **Brian Maye**, *Arthur Griffith* (1997); **J.L. Hyland**, *James Connolly* (1997); **Pauric Travers**, *Eamon de Valera* (1994); and **T.P. Coogan**, *Michael Collins* (1990).

Index